D0031448

HOW
LANCE
DOES IT

Put the Success Formula of a
Champion into Everything You Do

BRAD KEARNS

New York   Chicago   San Francisco   Lisbon   London   Madrid   Mexico City
Milan   New Delhi   San Juan   Seoul   Singapore   Sydney   Toronto

Library of Congress Cataloging-in-Publication Data

Kearns, Brad, 1965–
    How Lance does it : put the success formula of a champion into everything you do
/ Brad Kearns.
        p.   cm.
    Includes index.
    ISBN 0-07-147740-3 (alk. paper)
        1. Sports—Psychological aspects.   2. Athletes—Psychology.   3. Success.
4. Armstrong, Lance.   I. Title.

GV706.4.K425   2007
796'.01—dc22   2006022992

Copyright © 2007 by Brad Kearns. All rights reserved. Printed in the United States of America. Except as permitted under the United States Copyright Act of 1976, no part of this publication may be reproduced or distributed in any form or by any means, or stored in a database or retrieval system, without the prior written permission of the publisher.

1 2 3 4 5 6 7 8 9 10 11 12 13 14 15 16 17 18 19   DOC/DOC   0 9 8 7 6

ISBN-13: 978-0-07-147740-6
ISBN-10:   0-07-147740-3

Interior design by Nick Panos

McGraw-Hill books are available at special quantity discounts to use as premiums and sales promotions, or for use in corporate training programs. For more information, please write to the Director of Special Sales, Professional Publishing, McGraw-Hill, Two Penn Plaza, New York, NY 10121-2298. Or contact your local bookstore.

This book is printed on acid-free paper.

If you could have a day
To put on a pair of magic glasses
And see the world in a different way
Where human frailties like fear, insecurity, and anxiety were concepts
    difficult to grasp
Instead of obstacles in daily life
Where doing something that you loved and was the highest expression
    of your talents was a reality instead of a dream
Where you quickly eliminated unpleasant situations and people from
    your presence and the memories from your consciousness
And a positive attitude was not a fleeting gift mysteriously bestowed
    upon you or taken away based on life circumstances, but an
    empowering choice available even in the worst situations
Then you'd have a glimpse of what it's like to be Lance Armstrong

CONTENTS

ACKNOWLEDGMENTS

There are many people quoted here, all of whom deserve thanks for taking the time and offering excellent commentary—none more so than Lance Armstrong himself. When you spend even a few minutes in the presence of a popular public figure like Lance, the massive level of stimulation he faces in that position becomes clear. For someone disinclined, fame can be an energy-draining, negative phenomenon. Lance handles his role in life like a champ—both on and off the bike. He is perhaps the most difficult person in the world to pin down for an interview, but he's the most enjoyable and easiest interview imaginable—always 100 percent focused on giving clear and thoughtful answers. Once he even explained how to operate a new digital tape recorder I was fumbling with before we began!

Bart Knaggs and Bill Stapleton, the principals of Capital Sports and Entertainment, Lance's management firm in Austin, Texas, graciously gave me their blessing to pursue this project—a critical factor in its completion. Furthermore, as holders of the precious few backstage all-access passes to the Lance phenomenon, their unique insights for the text have greatly enhanced the end product.

The early drafts of this book might still be sitting on my hard drive if not for Farley Chase of the Waxman Literary Agency and Mark Weinstein of McGraw-Hill. They not only have given me the break that writers dream of but have been excellent strategists and supporters of my dreams. Many thanks to Mark for excellent developmental editing and tremendous patience with the project's timeline. Also thanks to the others who put the finishing touches on this project, including editors Marisa L'Heureux and Julia Anderson

Bauer of McGraw-Hill, copyeditor Laura Gabler, and designer Nick Panos.

Martin Brauns and Kevin Hayden of Interwoven, Inc., empowered and supported me to have a central role in a corporate relationship with Lance, a connection that made this book possible and was also great fun. Brauns provided excellent insights on applying Lance's success factors to the business world, something I hope many readers will find valuable. The work of writers Daniel Coyle (*Lance Armstrong's War*), Martin Dugard (*Chasing Lance*), Sally Jenkins (*It's Not About the Bike* and *Every Second Counts*, with Lance), Linda Armstrong Kelly (*No Mountain High Enough*), and Austin Murphy (*Sports Illustrated* feature articles) was greatly appreciated and valuable for this project. I particularly appreciate Linda Armstrong Kelly taking time out of her busy speaking schedule and putting aside her well-founded trepidation of discussing Lance for yet another book.

Other thanks go to my parents, Gail and Walter Kearns, and the entire Kearns and Dunigan families, who have encouraged and supported my dreams; Bob Babbitt, for the Hawaiian Bread and keen insights; Rip Esselstyn, for a great feel of the subject matter and the hospitality and gourmet dining when I was in Austin; Jimmy Riccitello, for his storytelling and sportsmanship; Ray Sidney, for the private air travel; and Craig Eigenbrod, Andrew MacNaughton, Kevin Pedrotti, Andy Robles, Bill Ross, Suzanne Schlosberg, Dan Squiller, Daniel Von Spanielle, Mark Sisson, Mike Greenberg, and Melvin Walters, for helpful writing and manuscript suggestions. I hope you enjoy the photos in this book, which have been contributed by Graham Watson, cycling's top photographer; Scott Clarke; and Nicole Cooke. The assistance of Luis Viggio, Stephanie McIlvain, and Kala Hoeschele with the photos was appreciated as well.

This book is about pursuing peak performance and being a champion in the broad sense of the word. Pursuant to that ideal, I strove to write with a positive attitude and a commitment to not compromise my health or well-being for the sake of the end product. My wife, Tracy, and children, Jack and Maria, are the greatest inspiration I could imagine to lead a healthy, balanced lifestyle. I hope that this book can contribute to yours.

Scott Clarke

INTRODUCTION

I woke up to the beautiful orange-yellow colors of a fall sunrise in the California desert. After driving away from the incredibly lush yet incredibly fake landscaping of my resort hotel/country club, I experienced my true surroundings: endless sand and succulent scrub brush—the only things that can naturally thrive in that hot, barren environment. Soon I arrived at a modest airstrip, checked my watch, and celebrated the rare occurrence of being on time for something. This was going to be a day where time was of the essence.

The Bermuda Dunes Airport in California's Coachella Valley (near Palm Springs) is an unlikely spot for a celebrity sighting, but sure enough, right on schedule, a white Cessna Citation X corporate jet—the "world's fastest corporate jet" with a cruising speed approaching six hundred miles per hour—appeared out of the sky. Everything about it was sleek and efficient, from its graceful dive from the sky to the strip to the way it made only a fraction of the annoying noise most commercial jets make.

The hatch door flipped open, marking the beginning of a crazy—that is to say, routine—day in the impossibly grand and complex life of Lance Armstrong. The occasion of Lance's visit to the desert was the 2001 convention of one of his corporate sponsors, Interwoven (a Silicon Valley software company). As the company's official Lance liaison (prerequisite for the position: having an old buddy from the triathlon circuit who later beats cancer and becomes the Tour de France champion), I was responsible for coordinating our allotted (per sponsorship contract) "one Lance day per year" to maximum advantage. With our top executives, customers, corporate partners, and sales staff gathered at the convention, it seemed like a great time to call in our ace from Texas to liven up the proceedings.

Before the convention, I huddled with Interwoven leaders to develop a wish list of events to be graced by Lance's presence for maximum impact. Then, with some friendly give-and-take with Lance's people—masters at protecting the extremely valuable commodities of their active athlete's time, energy, and comfort level—we crafted a detailed agenda.

The schmooze fest started with eighteen holes of golf. We planned for Lance to hopscotch in a chauffeured cart (not a bad gig for our young marketing assistant Maeve Naughton) all over the course, switching foursomes every three holes to directly play with twenty-four different people. After golf came a luncheon appearance, an hour-long autograph line, an employee dinner appearance, a top customer dinner appearance, and finally a scheduled flight departure at 9 P.M. Careful not to exhaust Lance, we also scheduled into the timeline "2:00 P.M.–4:15 P.M.: Relax at hotel."

Almost immediately after sending Lance the agenda, an e-mail came back from him inquiring whether we could squeeze in a bike ride during the downtime. As he explained, "Golf fucks up the body, so we'll need to pedal after." While I have yet to read this insight in an exercise physiology text, I would be reluctant to doubt its validity, considering the source. After all, on the Tour de France rest days (the twenty-plus-stage event always has a day or two in there of no racing, typically coinciding with a jet transfer if the next day's stage starts far away), every single rider in the event takes the opportunity to ride for up to three hours—not at a crawl but at a steady tempo—"so the body doesn't shut down and you keep your legs open as much as possible," wrote former U.S. professional rider Dylan Casey on his blog. Whatever, I thought. I guess we'll have to keep our minds open as much as possible, too.

I contacted Greg Klein, my buddy in the desert, asking him if he might be able to rearrange his schedule on late notice for a midday ride with a certain "very well-known professional cyclist." This would be on the lowdown, of course, to avoid a potential scene that might disrupt our timeline.

The October 9 outing happened to fall on Greg's birthday, and he came through with borrowed mountain bikes, caravan transportation for our small group, and golden tickets for two of his training partners.

The quick trip from the convention hotel to our trailhead was hastened en route by a cell phone call from an impatient Lance, in the trailing car, to Greg, in the lead car. "Hey, Greg, I hear it's your birthday. Happy birthday!" "Uh, who is this?" "It's Lance. Now what the hell is taking so long, and can we get to the trails any faster?" Feeling the heat of the yellow jersey chasing him, Greg bobbed and weaved through a shortcut down residential streets, and we soon reached the trailhead. We were at the foot of the incredibly steep mountains that rise from the Coachella Valley floor, near the famed Palm Springs Aerial Tramway, which whisks passengers 5,873 vertical feet into the San Jacinto Mountains in only two and a half miles.

After an eight-second warm-up in the parking lot, we ascended Dunn Fire Road, which climbs seven hundred feet in the first mile. On a grade this steep, one false move on the slippery dirt would send you jumping off your bike with all momentum lost. Not having done a serious ride in months, I was maxed out immediately. It wasn't very hot, but the muscle tension from the effort reverberated throughout my body, making my head feel like it was about to explode. My muscles soon adapted, however, and I fell into somewhat of a rhythm. After a few more minutes, I felt a second wind arrive; my breathing relaxed and pedaling cadence quickened slightly. Instead of fighting the dirt, my bike tires tracked effortlessly.

It was certainly not a race, but it felt reassuring to pull away from the pack (Lance was probably talking to someone behind, just warming up). I theorized that my years of hard training many years before had left an impressive residue of fitness in my body. Where was Lance anyway? As soon as I turned my head to glance backward, Lance let go of the rear of my seat, which he had been pushing up the trail. As he playfully accelerated past me, urging me to "Come on!" the tension immediately returned to my legs, and I had to fight my way up the rest of the climb.

Mercifully, the grade lessened briefly as we reached a treeless high valley offering direct exposure to the increasing power of the afternoon sun. After brief instructions from our guide at a trail fork, we took off on a beautiful single-track switchback climb, and Lance quickly drifted out of sight. As we continued to climb, our small group became separated from the effort, and we each engaged in our respective solo battles against the elements of elevation gain, desert heat, and a slick, sandy trail. As is often the case when endurance athletes get caught up in the rhythm and exhilaration of a long climb, we continued on well past our planned turnaround time. Usually this is no biggie, but in this case I had a few interested parties back at the hotel—namely, my employers—who were counting on me to ensure the Lance show ran on schedule literally to the minute.

I yelled to Lance in vain a few times and then realized that not only was he out of earshot but I was dealing with a force more powerful than a corporate appearance timeline. I was dealing with someone who loved riding his bike perhaps more than anyone else in the world and who was so accomplished at it that a hectic trip to pedal up a steep mountain served as a refreshing break from an incredibly stressful day as the recipient of an endless procession of energy-draining glad-handers, "quick story" tellers, and autograph seekers. Just as we saw on TV in France year after year in July, this was a machine in action that could not slow down or be stopped.

Here we were in October—as deep as you can get into his off-season—and Lance was hammering out of sight up a climb of several thousand feet. At the end of the ride, I commented to him that the winner of the next year's Tour de France had just been revealed to me. If Lance kicked everyone's butt the previous summer and was still showing tremendous fitness, motivation, and excitement to ride a bike during a time of year when even the most devoted pros have their bikes hanging from the rafters, how could anyone close the gap when the time came to get serious?

By the time we returned to the hotel, cleaned up, and got Lance into his hot seat, the autograph line had been kept waiting for an hour. I imagined a pink slip conversation with my boss: "Hey, got a sec? Let's go over here where it's quieter. So, you had a fun ride? Great, glad you got out there. Anyway, . . ." Instead, Kevin Hayden was all smiles, noting how Lance's tardiness "heightened the antic-ipation and excitement" of the autograph line. I guess celebrity magic rubs off on everyone around them. I wasn't the careless jerk who made Lance late; I was the facilitator of a bold expedition into the desert where Lance got "lost" on a bike ride! The story became a good icebreaker for those reaching the front of the line. And it wasn't really a lie when you define *lost* in the metaphysical sense.

Lance's secret weapon is not his genetic gifts or his killer instinct, for these endowments are shared by many of his competitors. Instead, it is his pure joy for living life and riding his bicycle. Imag-ine a top athlete during an exhausting fish-out-of-water corporate sponsor day in the off-season. Not many would want to squeeze in a tough workout during their precious downtime. Instead, they would probably choose eating a proper meal, relaxing, and sum-moning the energy to "get through" the rest of the obligation. As everyone he touched during these events can attest, Lance was in the moment, enjoying himself and his company at all times. Devel-oping the ability to go with the flow and enjoy every experience that life has to offer, even when things don't go exactly as desired or hoped for, is the essence of "how Lance does it."

The Rain Jacket

Lance Armstrong's approach to life is remarkably simple and clean, devoid of the psychological "issues" that make life a bitch for ordi-nary people. It just so happens that he became the ultimate sports celebrity, so the world has been able to deeply appreciate the results generated when he did what he loved on his bicycle.

The qualities that make Lance a great champion are a mysterious blend of genetics, background, attitude, and behavior molded by years of life experience. We will have a ball analyzing the particulars to bring meaning and generate inspiration from his example. Yet for Lance, everything must remain ridiculously simple. No one ever won the Tour de France by contemplating winning the Tour de France.

"When it's raining, I just put on a rain jacket and go." This was Lance's metaphoric answer to the question of how he dealt with vicious treatment at the hands of the European cycling media, who dogged him with unsubstantiated drug rumors for the duration of his Tour de France reign. There is simply nothing that can compromise Lance's positive attitude and total focus on his goals—whether it's literally inclement weather or the emotional storms that come from being a celebrity, team leader, and top dog in the high-pressure world of professional cycling.

"WHEN IT'S RAINING, I JUST PUT ON A RAIN JACKET AND GO."

—Lance Armstrong

Close your eyes for a second and imagine Lance waking up, looking outside, seeing rain, getting dressed appropriately, and heading out the door to train without hesitation. Behind this simple but highly symbolic image lie secrets that his competitors and everyday folk would kill for. You might not face a six-hour training ride in the freezing rain of Europe in February nor newspaper headlines that attack your character and accuse you of the worst sporting transgressions. However, each of us faces the "bad weather" of stress, negative emotions, and personal conflict in our daily lives. Do you put on a rain jacket and carry on? Or do you complain, explain, and blame?

One thing that becomes clear when you learn about Lance's story is his total refusal to consider any alternative but the best: survival, perfect preparation, victory, good sportsmanship, total honesty, and giving to something bigger than himself in the cancer community. Lance's story is pure Hollywood. He and his mom brazenly take on the world. He becomes a precocious world champion, gets cancer and nearly loses everything, and then comes back to achieve a victory so profound that he transcends his sport to become the American icon of hope. However, you would have to cast someone else as Lance for the movie, for Lance himself has no "glam factor."

As an athlete, Lance was much more like a surgeon than a flamboyant crowd pleaser. There was no unnecessary waste of emotions, no empty rhetoric with high shock value, no anxiety whatsoever with carrying on his back the hopes of an entire team (an enterprise that grew to sixty-plus employees and a budget of more than $15 million annually) and an entire country in striving to win the toughest individual athletic event on earth.

Lance's seven Tour de France victories were a testament to his mechanical preparation and refusal to let outside influences demoralize or distract him. With such a focused approach, he was able to perform successfully even while surrounded by a pandemonium that dwarfed anything other athletes have faced. Think of screaming Super Bowl or World Series fans unrestrained by stadium seats so that they may swarm the edges of the playing field and scream or spit in an athlete's face. Repeat the scenario every day for three weeks, and you end up with the estimated fifteen million roadside spectators in the Tour de France, enough to fill three hundred World Series stadiums.

It's easy to forget context when talking with Lance. In our interviews for this book, it felt like I was in casual conversation with an old friend about sports and life instead of having discussions—booked after months of waiting for a spot on his calendar—with one of the world's most recognizable and beloved athletes, one who achieved the greatest comeback in the history of sports, becoming the greatest cyclist of all time.

Lance is not the least bit self-important, long-winded, introspective, or mystical—he's just simple and straightforward. Of course, therein lies his secret. To be exposed to Lance's unique perspective may be particularly valuable because many of us struggle with an overly complex, self-absorbed approach to life. When things do not unfold exactly how we want and we get bogged down by mental demons like insecurity, peer pressure, and emotional baggage, we lose—whether it's a bike race or an attempt to live a happy life.

Many of us have read personal growth or self-help books before, each with an interesting take on how to achieve happiness, personal power, wealth, balance, peak performance, leadership—whatever the particular hook is. In fact, one could spend a lifetime sitting around and reading book after book—filling the eager mind with winning strategies and success acronyms while accomplishing nothing. Alternatively, you could set a goal that you would love to pursue and achieve, figure out precisely what it takes to achieve it, and head down that path with no hesitation or wasted energy.

The insights you get from Lance in this book are simple and clear. Not once in my interviews did I need him to elaborate or clarify a comment; nor did I struggle conceptually to interpret the meaning of his comments. The twists and turns that are normally taken during conversation were absent. That's because twists and turns typically come from gossip, rationalizing, ego demands, and analysis ad nauseam. Lance has no time or energy for this, probably because he has trained so hard and kept such a busy schedule for years.

At the end of one of our first conversations, I was left with a strange feeling when I turned off the tape recorder; it was the exact same feeling I had at the finish line of a prestigious triathlon competition that I had won after a long slump. Absolutely free of mental or physical struggle, I blew the field away effortlessly. And while I was elated at the finish line, I also felt a tinge of frustration. How was this so easy? Why can't it be like this every time?

It can be. If you can become sufficiently motivated and inspired (perhaps by this book or by reflecting for a moment on your own awesome potential) to quickly discard the drama and the baggage that drags you down, success can come easily. However, it often requires getting out of your own way. Lance's well-chronicled cancer survivor to champion cyclist story is a message of hope and believing in yourself. While I will set forth a template of attitude and behavior strategies to connect you with Lance's winning example, the rest is up to you. Unlike many popular culture know-it-alls, Lance does not profess to know any secrets beyond working hard and living strong. He inspires by example, the most powerful method of all.

Interwoven marketing manager Kathleen Means observes, "I think the way many people react to Lance is weird. It seems they want him to be perfect, to be their savior for cancer or hero for their kids. He is most certainly not perfect and has even very visibly 'failed' with his love relationships. I think he should be admired for having the focus to accomplish what he has, for that is an area that most people are severely lacking. What Lance has that you and I usually don't is focus."

The Lance Armstrong Success Factors

The concept of the Lance Armstrong success factors came to me in a burst of inspiration on the heels of that illuminating day spent with Lance in the desert during his off-season in 2001. After collapsing in a heap that evening and flying back home to resume my sane and predictable life the following morning, I realized that I had enjoyed a backstage glimpse of the forces behind the Tour de France champion that the world saw.

Watching Lance leave his competitors behind on the high mountains of the Tour de France are special moments that we have been privileged to enjoy repeatedly during his seven-year reign in the yellow jersey. There are important lessons to learn from observing the heat of battle and the glory of victory, but I believe that even richer insights and inspiration come about when you go backstage and discover the nature of the components that lead to the grand, onstage performance.

The purpose of *How Lance Does It* is to help you understand the attitude and behavior qualities that have made Lance Armstrong a champion and to show you how to apply them to your own peak performance goals to realize the highest expression of your talents. By taking a closer look at how Lance has conducted his cycling career and at his stance and opinions on a variety of peak performance–related topics, we will zero in on just what it takes to become a great champion. I will detail four distinct Lance Armstrong success factors, each with a separate chapter, as follows.

Success Factor 1: Positive Attitude

Lance has an intensely positive attitude about life, the key to overcoming difficult circumstances like cancer and winning the toughest bike race in the world seven years in a row. He constantly maintains a winning environment for himself and everyone around him by choosing to interpret his past experiences and present circumstances in a positive manner.

Success Factor 2: Clarity of Purpose

Lance had a deep conviction and commitment to realize his potential as a cyclist, which resulted in his winning the Tour de France every year from 1999 through 2005. He was motivated by his love of cycling and desire to give his absolute best effort after surviving cancer and being given a second chance in life. In daily life, Lance consistently displayed the work ethic, focus, and prioritization skills that matched his clear life purpose every day. He was willing to make the tremendous sacrifices necessary to become a champion and prevent outside influences (competitors, the distractions of celebrity life, and so on) from impeding him.

Success Factor 3: Specialized Intelligence

Lance has extremely high intelligence narrowly applied and perfectly suited to his chosen endeavor as a pro cyclist. He developed his specialized intelligence by learning and improving from mistakes, cultivating an intuitive approach to training and life decisions, and adopting a big-picture perspective about his athletic goals to account for all performance variables.

Success Factor 4: Pure Confidence

Lance's greatest source of confidence was "doing the work"—preparing fully and competing in high-pressure situations. He was focused on achieving peak performance and was not afraid to lose. This pure confidence transcends external variables that cause many to succumb to the negative influences of competitive pressure and the expectations of others.

I will support the success factor theory with never-before-published anecdotes from my extensive interviews with Lance, those in his tight inner circle, and other key observers. We will see where Lance heads in the future, but it's no doubt that he is poised to apply his success factors in whatever direction he chooses—cancer advocacy, working with the Discovery Channel cycling team he partly owns, business and corporate sponsorship affairs, or just being a mellow dad raising three kids in Austin, Texas. You, too, can apply these success factors to pursuits such as raising a family, running a business, pursuing an education, competing in cycling competitions, uncovering dinosaur bones, repairing shoes, or any other endeavor you might have a passion for.

Graham Watson, grahamwatson.com

PEELING THE ONION
WHO IS LANCE ARMSTRONG?

You may have read some or much of the extensive commentary in books and magazine articles about the character of Lance Armstrong—his cancer survivor–influenced commitment to live life to the fullest, his work ethic, his commanding presence as a team leader, and his fierce competitive nature. Many, many people have weighed in on the subject, offering everything from clever and revealing sound bites to banal clichés. *Sports Illustrated* writer Austin Murphy, who has covered many of Lance's exploits for the magazine, took a good crack at characterizing Lance when he wrote:

> While it may be tempting to put Armstrong in the category of such icy, aloof winners as Ted Williams and Joe DiMaggio—sometimes surly champions willing to jettison civility, politesse and friendships in pursuit of their art—Lance's case is more complicated. Stern taskmaster though he may be, he is also charming, witty and kindhearted. No athlete in history has used his celebrity to do more good: The Lance Armstrong Foundation has raised a stunning $85 million to date. He is more Albert Schweitzer than Albert Belle.

While Lance's intriguing profile has received a lot of attention, I believe that there are still many more layers of the onion left to peel.

Over the past nearly twenty years, I have observed the Lance phenomenon mostly from afar. But I am also privileged to have had some of my own rich personal experiences with Lance that have brought with them awesome, life-altering lessons.

In attempting to get to know someone (or perhaps write a book about someone), it's valuable to look closely for character-revealing insights. These insights are difficult to come by in a world where we are essentially acting out roles that match our daily responsibilities. The more structured the situation, the heavier the acting and the more difficult it is to see behind the theater masks that we all wear for our daily roles. Consider your typical sports interview or press conference—what a royal waste of time! We get thoughtless questions, disingenuous answers, rote spewing of sound bites ("I respect my opponent and am focused on my own game plan, just going out there and giving my best effort." "If we perform to our capabilities and work together as a team, we can win this thing." "Hey, we're just happy to be here, you know, but it sure feels great to win because we worked so hard all year." Blah blah blah.), and only rare departures from the soft-shoe routine. Truly personal questions are out of bounds as are truly vulnerable responses.

Ditto for a job interview—two people engaged in a familiar back-and-forth of the right questions and the right answers. When I worked in human resources, we'd strategize about the best questions to ask to maximize the insights gained from a job interview and avoid "bad hires." Sure, open-ended inquiries and hypothetical situation challenges help determine someone's experience and ability to think on his or her feet, but they don't take you outside the confinements of the game.

I joked to my coworkers that we should launch booby traps in an attempt to penetrate the veil of the interview game. For example, what if you put the CEO at the reception desk for the candidate's arrival and then had the CEO purposefully hassle the candidate a little ("I'm sorry, your name again? Here to see whom again?")? Would the person be dismissive or brusque on the assumption that the receptionist wasn't important? How would a candidate respond to repeated interruptions while she was talking? Insights gained from behavior in these situations would be more revealing than the typical "tell me about your last position" mumbo jumbo.

Psychology texts describe a distinction between our basic self and our conscious self. The basic self is the source of our raw instincts; subconscious thoughts, needs, and desires; and the unrestrained childlike expression of emotions. The conscious self is responsible for making decisions, governing our daily behavior, and regulating the urges and needs of the basic self. As sports psychologist James Loehr points out in his book *Stress for Success*, we spend as much as 90 percent of our time modifying our behavior and emotions to fit what we consider to be appropriate for the situation. This is not a bad thing—in fact, it is vital to getting along in the world. The conscious self guides you to be patient and polite all day at work, while the basic self takes over when you walk into your house and snap at your wife for no reason—except to release the stress and tension of modifying your behavior and emotions all day for the sake of a sedate workplace.

Particularly in the realms of big-time athletics and business, where poker faces are the norm and vulnerability is a fatal flaw, character-revealing insights are vital to sifting through the acting bullshit and potentially getting an edge over the competition. The late Mark McCormack, founder of the global sports marketing powerhouse IMG, wrote in his book *What They Don't Teach You at Harvard Business School* that the golf course was his favored venue for character revelations, saying, "You can tell more about how a person will react in a business situation from one round of golf than in a hundred hours of meetings." Out on the course, insights flow freely for many reasons: the frustrating nature of the game, the fact that athletic competition magnifies the lessons of success and failure and our reaction to them, and, finally, because it represents a vulnerable fish-out-of-water arena for interaction with business associates. Consider how you might obtain personality insights and predict business-arena behavior from golf partners who engage in negative self-talk, are surreptitious about their competitive intensity, cheat on the scorecard, and so forth.

> ## "YOU CAN TELL MORE ABOUT HOW A PERSON WILL REACT IN A BUSINESS SITUATION FROM ONE ROUND OF GOLF THAN IN A HUNDRED HOURS OF MEETINGS."
>
> —Mark McCormack

Kindling for the Fire

Lance's legendary drive and killer instinct have been well chronicled though often inaccurately connected to the misfortunes he has suffered in his life. There is an important nuance to understand between dwelling on failure and allowing it to fuel you for peak performance. For example, we know that Lance felt like an outcast in his snobby high school and struggled with disappointing father figures during his upbringing. Yet Lance says that he wastes little time pondering these hardships of his past, instead offering glowing praise for his dynamo mom, Linda Armstrong Kelly, who raised him alone, struggling with minimal economic resources.

Kelly's autobiography, *No Mountain High Enough*, is a tale of survival and turning one adversity after another into opportunities for personal growth and a strengthened bond with her family—that is, her and Lance. Pregnant at sixteen and kicked out of the house is not a winning hand, but Linda had some aces up her sleeve with a winning attitude.

> Having Lance very, very young and realizing that he was going to define my life and my future was probably the best thing that ever happened to me. Lance was my salvation in my life. He gave me purpose. I set out to give him the things that I didn't have. Not material things, but the things that would allow him to someday spread his wings and make a contribution to society.
>
> I will always find that optimistic way out of a bad situation. You want to take me on, take me on—because *I will win!* There were certain realities in our life that couldn't be changed. We could sit around and cry about it, or we could find a way around the roadblocks. Our answer to every setback, sorrow, and upheaval has always been to push back, try harder, be smarter. We weren't afraid of failing—only of stopping, of giving up. Losing is worthwhile if you learn something from it, but quitting is the defeat of hope.

"HAVING LANCE VERY, VERY YOUNG AND REALIZING THAT HE WAS GOING TO DEFINE MY LIFE AND MY FUTURE WAS PROBABLY THE BEST THING THAT EVER HAPPENED TO ME."

—Linda Armstrong Kelly

Lance, too, famously places his cancer ordeal entirely in a positive light, going so far as to echo his mom's quote that it was "the best thing that ever happened to me." Many might gain illumination from that simple insight—dwelling on the emotional and physical scars of your past is not a recipe for success or happiness.

Troy Hoidal was one of Lance's original sponsors and a big brother–type mentor during Lance's teenage years on the triathlon circuit, when Lance and I first crossed paths. He remembers, "I never heard Lance complain about anything. I know he was not too happy to be called 'the Kid' [an unimaginative nickname that didn't stick very well on the triathlon circuit]. He always thought of himself as a man. He was not very happy with John Tomac [the top mountain bike racer in the world who later had a moderately successful career on the road in Europe] or Greg LeMond [three-time Tour de France champion] in those days, either. These were the two guys at the head of their classes and Lance wanted to join up. But neither gave him the time of day. I know this drove him. Lance would never dwell on his defeats; he would always be thinking ahead to the next race and how his training would need to change. Deep inside he knew one day his time would come."

> ## "OUR ANSWER TO EVERY SETBACK, SORROW, AND UPHEAVAL HAS ALWAYS BEEN TO PUSH BACK, TRY HARDER, BE SMARTER."
> —Linda Armstrong Kelly

You can generate tremendous positive energy and motivation from misfortune and perceived slights—if you process them properly. Lance was a master at creating controversy and tension to fuel a sufficiently sized motivational fire for the duration of his career. For example, for the 1999 Tour (his first victory), he wanted to prove to the world that he could come back from cancer. For his second Tour victory, in 2000, he wanted to prove that he could beat top contenders Jan Ullrich and Marco Pantani, who had both skipped '99. In 2001 and 2002 doping allegations gained momentum, giving Lance something to lash out against. In 2003 he had to try and match the record of five Tour victories. In 2004 he aimed to break through the mysterious invisible barrier that had thwarted each of the previous five-time winners (Jacques Anquetil, Eddy Merckx, Bernard Hinault, and Miguel Indurain), who attempted to win a sixth and never did. For his final Tour in 2005, Lance naturally had to go out on top and win again.

No Thanks, Hollywood

It's hard to really know celebrities because their lives are so magnified that they become distorted. The image obscures the true person—something that many celebrities leverage to increase their popularity! When Lance announced his separations from Kristin, the mother of his three children, in 2003 and then from Sheryl Crow in 2006, the general consensus among his fans seemed to be, "Wow, what happened?" What happened was real life playing out with real people, which is not always pretty or perfect.

The goal here is not to contribute to the soap opera phenomenon that surrounds public figures like Lance today but to reveal attitude and behavior insights about a great champion that can inspire you to lead a better life. Along those lines, it's important to dispel some flawed perceptions that I believe exist about Lance. Lance is an extremely intense and driven competitor, but is he a "ruthless dictator" as some have characterized him? I guess it depends on your perspective. As the leader of a substantial business empire in a very competitive arena, Lance is capable of making the hard decisions that can and have created enemies and negative feelings from those left in his wake. Instead of taking the easy way out and avoiding conflict and criticism, Lance is an incurable straight shooter. Those who can respect and appreciate that are welcomed, while those who can't get frozen out or even slapped with a lawsuit if necessary.

Lance took the opportunity at his farewell speech on the Champs-Élysées after his final Tour de France victory in 2005 to slam "those who don't believe." He was largely referring to the members of the European media who have hounded his career and stressed his personal life with drug abuse rumors for the duration of his run at the top of what they considered to be "their" sport. It seems that Lance's penchant for directness and honesty instead of strategic political correctness has led to much of the severe criticism he has received. Perhaps if he had sucked up to the media since day one—when instead of celebrating the greatest comeback in the history of sports (his 1999 Tour de France victory), some preposterously speculated that the drugs his cancer was treated with had made him "superhuman"—they would have laid off him for the next six years.

> INSTEAD OF TAKING THE EASY WAY OUT
> AND AVOIDING CONFLICT AND CRITICISM,
> LANCE IS AN INCURABLE STRAIGHT SHOOTER.

This may be a turnoff to some. After all, the plain-vanilla image of golf superstar Tiger Woods is worshipped by millions—and he no doubt worships the millions that come to him for playing the corporate America image game. While Tiger has done a whole lot of good for his charitable causes, he has rarely uttered anything controversial, nor stuck his neck out for any cause that might pose a risk to his clean image. I'm not saying he needs to; for me it's enough to watch him do his thing on the golf course and let him go back to his $22 million yacht (oxymoronically named *Privacy*) in peace. I think we all can and should do without the fluff, gossip, and superfluous celebrity hero worship that the media serve up.

"Lance is not an actor," says Interwoven marketing manager Kathleen Means. "I remember when he arrived at our San Francisco Convention in 2000, fresh off the transcontinental flight from the Sydney Olympics. We rushed him into a room to sign five hundred books (in a record time of seventeen minutes, forty seconds!) and a bunch of posters and shirts. I thought, this is insane, he must be exhausted. What was interesting was that he didn't really try and hide the fact that he was tired to the small group of people in his suite," remembers Means. "He didn't waste any energy trying to be polished, because it was not his goal to be polished. He just mustered the energy to get the job done in a pretty straightforward, no-nonsense way. He was the same in his speech at the convention to a thousand people. He chose not to be too slick and instead came off completely nonintimidating. I suppose that is why people are drawn to him."

"HE DIDN'T WASTE ANY ENERGY TRYING TO BE POLISHED, BECAUSE IT WAS NOT HIS GOAL TO BE POLISHED. HE JUST MUSTERED THE ENERGY TO GET THE JOB DONE IN A PRETTY STRAIGHTFORWARD, NO-NONSENSE WAY."

—Kathleen Means

Two and a Half Hours

In 2001 I witnessed Lance and his agent Bill Stapleton hastily depart from a big-budget photo shoot for a major sponsor before the director was finished, because it ran over the scheduled time. The crew was exasperated that Lance would just up and bail on them with still a few key shots left to take. However, Lance honored his contract of appearing (and being a hardworking, agreeable, and infectiously positive subject) for the duration of the two-and-a-half-hour shoot. He had every right to expect the crew to honor their side of the contract to wrap up in that time frame.

I gained some interesting insights chatting with a production assistant at the shoot. "Today's shoot is an eight-hour operation that we are squeezing into two and a half," she told me. "We shoot every other athlete for the catalog in eight hours, and I mean *every* other athlete—the biggest names in sports." She explained how much easier the pace is on these days, with the extended catered lunch and plenty of downtime between shots to relax and strategize. This is not a luxury Lance could or wanted to afford during his career. She also mentioned that some of their other big-time athletes were high-maintenance—to use a polite two-word description instead of her one-word profanity—and how much more stressful these shoots were because of the bad attitudes posed by the subjects.

Ponder this for a moment if you want to understand what Lance is all about and how he differs from his brethren in the athletic world. On one hand you have two and a half hours of intensity, focus, and fun, exciting hard work. And when the clock strikes twelve, his carriage (or, in this case, the Citation X jet) is out of there. On the other hand you have a full day babysitting a high-maintenance character, politely begging for cooperation to get the shots you need, and trying not to ruffle feathers in the process. Which athlete would you rather work with?

JOE'S COOL

Maeve Naughton clarifies that she was not actually Lance's golf cart chauffeur at the Palm Springs convention's golf event. "Naturally, I was nervous to meet Lance and even rehearsed what I was going to say when we met. Everyone was milling about at the golf course, unpacking and arranging the clubs on carts and so on. Suddenly, we were face-to-face: 'Hi. I'm Maeve. I'll be driving you around the golf course today.' To which he replied, 'No, I'll be driving you. Give me the keys.'

"For the next five-plus hours we got along great," Naughton remembers. "He was so easy to talk to and incredibly funny. I guess, having never met a famous person before, I expected him to be a bit more standoffish and serious, but he was quite the opposite. He asked me silly questions about corporate life and told me stories in return. Once he commanded me to look the other way when he had to pee in the bushes. He even gave me a nickname—Susie. In return I called him Joe. I quickly found out why Lance wanted to drive the cart; he thinks a golf course is a 4 × 4 rally track! He'd leave the path and fly over hills as fast as he could, trying to get air. Among other things I learned from Lance, golf carts are not built for off-road use."

Most professional athletes train for a few hours a day at the most, doing things that are not as physically demanding as the massive miles accumulated by a professional cyclist year-round. Because Lance had to constantly devote hours and hours to physically exhausting training, he had no choice but to compress the timelines of everything else he did during his cycling career. If he was not attentive to this, he could not honor his tremendous and potentially conflicting commitments to the cancer community, to his personal and family life, and to winning the Tour de France. If you can't understand that position, he may very well leave you disappointed.

The CSE Boys

Anyone who has seen the Lance machine operate up close will agree that this is an incredibly tight, efficient, and highly disciplined operation. You would certainly not expect milquetoast supporting cast members. The main players on the business side of the Lance operation, Bart Knaggs and Bill Stapleton, are far from it. Stapleton and Knaggs, as principals of Capital Sports and Entertainment (CSE), which handles Lance's business affairs and owns the Discovery Channel Pro Cycling Team, operate somewhat out of the public spotlight, but they are champions in their own right. Stapleton was a member of the 1988 U.S. Olympic Swim Team, a multiple national champion, and ranked number two in the world in the 200-meter individual medley, one of the most grueling events in swimming. He is the one who has sold the Lance brand to corporate America, thereby helping Lance transcend the minor sport (in the United States) of cycling to become an icon in the pattern of Michael Jordan and Tiger Woods. He, as Lance's agent and attorney, has also largely shouldered the monumental burden of dealing

"AMONG OTHER THINGS I LEARNED FROM LANCE, GOLF CARTS ARE NOT BUILT FOR OFF-ROAD USE."

—Maeve Naughton

with a never-ending stream of litigation relating to the accusations of Lance using performance-enhancing drugs.

Knaggs was the Texas State Champion and Category I racing cyclist (the highest-ranking class in U.S. amateur cycling, indicating a national-caliber competitor just below professional level) when he first met Lance. He founded Trajecta, an artificial intelligence software company, out of graduate school (this despite no formal computer science, software engineering, or other technical training), building it and selling it five years later. As told in some detail in Lance's autobiography *It's Not About the Bike*, Knaggs was integral to Armstrong's treatment as a cancer patient. In 2004 Knaggs took the lead role for CSE, stepping in and assuming management of Lance's team (then title-sponsored by the U.S. Postal Service). He helped guide CSE in bringing sponsors like Discovery Channel and AMD Technology on board and developing ThePaceline.com, an Internet-based fan club that in 2006 had reached 250,000 members.

Knaggs's creative, entrepreneurial mind drove innovations like putting product into programming. For example, popular Discovery Channel documentaries like "Chasing Lance" highlight sponsors' equipment and technology used for the team's training and competition. This is light-years ahead of the antiquated strategy of slapping a corporate logo on a team jersey and hoping for "impressions" seen during television broadcasts. Together, Stapleton and Knaggs have leveraged an incredible natural resource—Lance Armstrong's cycling career—into a dramatic success.

Stapleton comments on the benefits of working for and with Lance: "My relationship with Lance has made me better; he's made everyone around him better. What makes Lance such a great client is that he's so demanding, direct, and forthright. If he's pissed off about something, he doesn't carry it around. He doesn't talk about it six months later when he's firing me. He calls me up and says, 'You fucked up.'

"What makes me good is that I'll acknowledge mistakes and I don't have any hang-ups about being forthright with him," Stapleton explains. "One thing that I've never forgotten is that I work for Lance. I think the people who have had difficulty became caught up in 'Lance world'—the celebrity world. They wanted to become his peer—riding bikes or doing business. I've never forgotten that I'm his bitch when it comes to getting stuff done. And I'm cool about it. What's interesting today is that we are becoming peers in one context. He's a shareholder in Capital Sports and Entertainment; he's seen the company grow and wants to be a part of it. We have an office for him down the hall where he can come in to work!" says Stapleton. From its inception in 1995, when the then Capital Sports Ventures operated out of Stapleton's living room with one client, CSE today occupies an Austin, Texas, riverfront high-rise and represents numerous other athletic and musical talents and produces large-scale events like the popular Austin City Limits concert festival.

Stapleton continues, "You can't spend time in this business and not understand that there is a client and a person who services the client. You have to check your ego at the door. The reason we've made it for eleven years is that we've had some pretty forthright conversations on both ends—what worked, what didn't work, what we need to do to make it work. We haven't had many difficulties, but when things need to be discussed, we put them on the table and get through them."

These dynamics are a rarity in the business world, particularly with the agent-client relationship model. "When people can't be forthright, relationships deteriorate," Stapleton explains. "Someone might whisper in his ear, 'Hey, Lance, IMG [the world's largest sports marketing and athlete representation firm] can do this and that for you.' If Lance thinks I'm not doing enough or getting him enough, he'll tell me. Then we will have a frank discussion about it, where I'll say, 'How much do you want to do? How hard do you want to work? Here's what we can do.' And we'll continue moving forward."

Bush League

This direct and forthright internal dynamic extends out to Lance and CSE's business relationships as well. Once I brokered a deal whereby Lance would become the keynote speaker of an awards banquet for exceptional high school students. In return for delivering him at half of his normal six-figure speaking fee, Interwoven would become the title sponsor of this grand event, held in an arena seating thousands. Lance's appearance would fulfill an obligation in his Interwoven contract, and everyone would win. As was customary for every Lance event, Stapleton and I carefully negotiated and scripted the timeline down to the minute for the two-hour appearance. For example, if the banquet folks initially wanted Lance to "mingle at a cocktail reception: thirty minutes," that would be streamlined into a twenty-minute structured autograph line at the reception, a much more comfortable endeavor than mixing and making small talk. At last, Stapleton got Lance to sign off, and I presented the client with the final timeline.

Well, the young, ambitious representative of the awards production wanted to engage in a little more give-and-take. I explained to her that this was the final result of extensive effort, approved by Lance, and extremely unlikely to change. She persisted, rebuffing my explanations about the value of my middleman role, the sensitivity of reopening a negotiation, and the difference between Lance's time as an active professional athlete and the next keynote speaker choice—say, someone like Barbara Bush. She requested to speak directly to Stapleton. I politely gave her the phone number (hey, CSE is in the phone book anyway!) with a final word of caution.

Less than an hour later I received an e-mail from Stapleton that was five words in length: "too much hassle, we're out."

When I broke the news to the client, she started tripping through the five stages of grief: denial, anger, bargaining, depression—but not quite making it to acceptance. After all, this is not how the typical "We're paying this guy a lot of money!" game works. You know, hire someone or buy something, negotiate back and forth in an attempt to take as much time, energy, and other resources as possible from them for as little money as possible, and then carry on. As Stapleton has reminded me numerous times, "Lance needs to feel good about something or he won't do it. We need to have good juju [energy] with our deals."

In this case Lance and Stapleton put their money where their mouths were and walked away from what most would consider a nice annual salary for two hours of work, simply because of negative vibes about the initial negotiation. There is no doubt that Stapleton could have asserted his position and left the final schedule unchanged, and the client would have carried on (who do you think high school kids would rather see as a keynote speaker, Lance or Barbara—the eventual headliner?). However, the routine stresses and hassles of daily life and business relationships inhibit our ability to perform at our peak. They drain our energy, compromise our positive attitudes, and distract our focus. Lance simply cannot have these hassles in his life because of the magnitude of his goals and the need to protect his energy and his positive disposition.

We've all been in similar positions and plowed through the bad juju for the sake of getting a job, feeling guilty about letting someone down, avoiding conflict, making a few extra bucks, or other impure motivations. Whether you're an athlete entering a competition, unsure about your fitness level, or signing a business contract despite negative premonitions, blinded by a selfish focus on your potential upside, you frequently end up getting screwed one way or the other.

Jumping the Barricade

In the fall, Lance raced several times in the San Francisco Grand Prix, a circuit race through the city that closed out the competitive season and represented a rare chance to watch the Tour de France champ in action on American soil. One year, an acquaintance of mine who drove a couple hours to see the race reported back, "I'm sorry, but Lance Armstrong is an asshole." It seems he wiggled his way to a close-up view along the barricade of a bullpen where riders were assembling on their bikes behind the starting line.

ROUTINE STRESSES AND HASSLES OF
DAILY LIFE AND BUSINESS RELATIONSHIPS
INHIBIT OUR ABILITY TO PERFORM
AT OUR PEAK.

With Lance only a few feet away, the fan repeatedly called his name, drew eye contact, and asked him to autograph something in hand. Apparently Lance met his eye contact without acknowledgment and without signing the item. So that makes Lance an asshole. Here is a professional athlete, moments before the start of an extremely difficult and dangerous 108-mile race, and he is an asshole for not signing an autograph. I pulled a character-revealing insight from that story, but it was not about Lance.

In the twenty years I have known Lance, I have known him to be kind, sensitive, and extremely loyal to the people that show the same consideration to him. Jimmy Riccitello, a longtime pro triathlete and occasional winter training partner of Lance's in Tucson, shares some Lance observations. "One winter in Tucson, we rode basically every day for a month. I think people have this image of a big-shot athlete like Lance being a coddled person, but it's not like that. The guy works very hard and he is go, go, go all the time. Most professional athletes will go do a workout, then come home, put their feet up, and relax on the couch. Lance will come home from a ride and immediately start conducting business. And I don't mean 'business' like the next guy—running errands or whatever—but big-time, big decision, complicated business. Actually I shouldn't say 'after a ride' because when you train with Lance, he spends the first hour of the ride on his cell phone!"

Riccitello continues, "Lance has always been a loyal guy. At the Tour de France, he was extremely accommodating to me numerous times. In 2003 I was conducting a cycling camp nearby, so I rode down to the starting line one day with the vague hope of running into Lance. As I approached the team bus, it was surrounded by a sea of people—and Lance wasn't even there! They were just waiting in the hopes that he might show up later. I approached a guy wearing a U.S. Postal team shirt who was busy preventing the throng from climbing over the crowd-control barricades. I said, 'Hey, do me a favor. If you see Lance, tell him Jimmy Riccitello said hello.' The guy said he would try to pass along the message if he saw him later. I figured, 'Yeah, right, whatever. At least I tried.'

"Soon there was a big commotion as Lance and George Hincapie rode up and quickly entered the trailer. Pretty soon the guy I spoke to comes out of the trailer and starts scanning the crowd. I'm thinking, 'Wow, he must be looking for me!' I pushed my way up to the front and the guy says, 'Hey, come on over,' so I leaped over the barricade. I don't speak much French, but the gendarmes were not happy about this, thinking that others would be inspired to pull the same stunt. People started throwing all kinds of shit at me for him to sign, but I didn't pick any of it up.

"I spent a few moments with Lance inside the bus," remembers Riccitello. "Lance had just gotten his butt kicked the day before, but he assured me that it was a fluke and that he was going to win that day. Here is a guy, struggling with his form, in the midst of all that craziness, and he still had time for me. And look, I'm just a guy who he met when he was sixteen years old and trained with once in a while. I can't say I'm a close friend of his. But even today, if I e-mail him, I'll get a response in three or four minutes. That's impressive to me," concludes Riccitello.

Lance's sportsmanship on the racecourse was impeccable, as is true for many other members of the tradition- and camaraderie-steeped pro cycling ranks. In the 2001 Tour, Lance's main rival, German rider Jan Ullrich, missed a curve on a steep descent and flew head over handlebars down an embankment. Lance immediately slowed his pace—and commanded others in the pack to do the same—until Ullrich caught up to him. When asked about his gesture after the race, Lance explained that he simply waited for Ullrich so that they could resume a fair race. Later in the stage, when the two were together on the final climb to the finish, Lance dropped him and rode away mercilessly, proving that it's OK to have a killer instinct and still be a good sport.

Unlike most sports heroes, Lance goes extra miles behind the scenes for the people who really deserve it—particularly children and families afflicted with cancer—without getting his ego and a superficial need for recognition involved. A 2005 *Sports Illustrated* feature story about the richest professional athletes and their charitable contributions was an embarrassment to the profession—a collectively very small percentage of their massive incomes are contributed to the charities. Sure, it's cool for a basketball player to pledge a thousand dollars to hurricane relief for every three-pointer he hits, but it equates to the middle-class American sending a check for forty cents. In contrast stand a few shining examples—including Lance, Andre Agassi, and Tiger Woods—who contribute massive amounts of money, time, and effort to their foundations and other charitable causes.

IT'S OK TO HAVE A KILLER INSTINCT AND STILL BE A GOOD SPORT.

As a high-profile figure who deserves a nomination for a "World's Busiest Man" award, Lance has undoubtedly left some people in his wake disappointed. It's hard to be in more than one place at a time, hard to make everyone happy, and hard to figure out exactly what the public wants and needs from its celebrities. My loose connection to the Lance machine has caused many people to reach out to me with heartrending requests to get an autographed item or e-mail from Lance on behalf of someone suffering from cancer.

After making a particularly passionate request for someone battling the final stages of brain cancer, I received an eye-opening message about the nature and magnitude of the Lance phenomenon from Bill Stapleton. As kindly and sensitively as possible, Stapleton related, "We receive hundreds of similar requests *every day*. It's impossible to fulfill them. We wish that people gain a connection and inspiration from Lance's books and his cycling performances—that will have to do."

Besides envisioning the massive pile of mail begging for Lance to touch, there is further symbolism to be drawn from Stapleton's statement. If a book is as close as you will ever get to Lance, maybe that should suffice. Take inspiration from Lance's words and example of how to live life to the fullest. Then go out and make a difference in the world and inspire others to do the same. In doing so, you will honor yourself and also Lance as an inspirational component to your success. With this arrangement, you are connected in a far more meaningful way than having an autographed photo hanging on your wall.

Graham Watson, grahamwatson.com

2

THE MYSTERY OF WHAT CONSTITUTES A CHAMPION

At my son's elementary school, a few of us athletic, competitive parents produce a Skyridge School Olympics competition several times a year. Here every kid in the school competes in a sprint and a distance race, receiving a time and a ranking in his or her grade. This format allows each kid to strive for personal improvement over the year and for the fastest to achieve distinction in a competitive arena. This is about as pure as sport can get: a group of kids who are uncoached, untrained, and uninfluenced by the pressures, expectations, and high stakes of organized higher-level sports. They compete in the most simple and straightforward of competitions—footraces—in a casual and fun environment during the school day.

One can gain fascinating crystal ball revelations from watching these kids in action. It was no different at my elementary school thirty years ago—those blessed with natural talent reveal themselves easily. They quickly ascend to the forefront of the athletic arena and have a high probability of remaining there through high school.

Nature, Nurture, and Mr. X

My dad likes to call professional athletes "freaks." While the American dream of having a successful career is theoretically open to most through education and hard work, the athletes we watch on TV truly are genetic freaks on a scale of one in a million. No amount of hard work will open these locker-room doors for someone lacking the requisite genetic gifts. Dad's coarse characterization was an effective influence on me to stay focused on my studies as a sports-obsessed teenager.

NO AMOUNT OF HARD WORK WILL OPEN THESE LOCKER-ROOM DOORS FOR SOMEONE LACKING THE REQUISITE GENETIC GIFTS.

The Genetic Rift

The most dramatic example of this genetic freak theory comes in the sport of running—both sprinting and distance competition. Here the top athletes come from a selection pool of millions spanning nearly every nation on the globe, virtually free of economic barriers or the lack of suitable venues or equipment in various cultures and regions. The "world's fastest human" (as the top 100-meter runner is traditionally called) has most certainly been discovered in a literal sense and is wearing the Olympic gold medal around his neck. By comparison, identifying the "world's best" golfer or skier needs to be qualified or considered a misnomer because relatively few have access to the more complex venues and equipment of these sports.

Instead of a cultural balance in the elite ranks, the sport of running is profoundly dominated by a small segment of the world population. As Jon Entine discusses at length in his fascinating book *Taboo: Why Black Athletes Dominate Sports and Why We're Afraid to*

Talk About It, the world's top male distance runners are heavily concentrated in an area of East Africa known as the Great Rift Valley adjacent to Lake Victoria. More specifically, the runners come from a group of tribes called the Kalenjin, who number only around one and a half million people. Entine calls this East African distance-running domination "the greatest per capita concentration of raw athletic talent in the history of the world." Sixty percent of the world's top distance-running marks are by runners of East African ancestry. Runners from one district called the Nandi, with a population of only five hundred thousand, win an amazing 20 percent of major international distance competitions.

Meanwhile, in the world of sprinting, athletes who trace their ancestry from West Africa have an almost complete stranglehold on the starting blocks and medal stands in championship events and the all-time performers list. While only 12 percent of the world's population has West African ancestry, members of this group claim 494 of the top 500 times in history (99 percent) in the 100-meter dash.

Today every men's running record from 100 meters to the marathon is held by an athlete of African ancestry (West African for 100, 200, and 400 meters, then North or East African for distances beyond that). The genetic component is obvious. Entine offers further support by contrasting the performances of the East Africans in sprinting, where the Kenyan record time ranks only around five thousandth on the all-time list and there is not a single distance runner of world-class ability with West African heritage. Scientists are hard at work unraveling this mystery. For example, one study identified a fat oxidation molecule that is more prominent in a group of African distance runners than in runners of other ancestry.

The Hood and the Country Club

Athletic potential may have a strong genetic influence but perhaps an even stronger cultural component. Top Kenyan distance runners

ATHLETIC POTENTIAL MAY HAVE A STRONG GENETIC INFLUENCE BUT PERHAPS AN EVEN STRONGER CULTURAL COMPONENT.

also happen to frequently train together in spartan camps with three-a-day workouts that are phenomenally difficult—well beyond those attempted by most elite runners from other countries. These Rift Valley runners have lived for generations at high altitude (developing naturally enriched blood for better oxygen-carrying capacity) in a culture where feet are still a key transportation mode. They have an excellent diet with staples like corn, beans, fruit, and vegetables—optimum for endurance training and recovery. Finally, they have an economic incentive to excel that dwarfs that of any non–third world athlete. An American collegiate distance runner pursuing a higher education leading to a comfortable and stable career will have a different perspective running laps around the track from an athlete from Kenya. Kenya is one of the poorest nations in the world, with an annual per capita income of $1,100 (source: the *World Factbook*), while the winner of the New York City marathon earns at least $100,000 (not counting time bonuses and sponsor bonuses). Kenya has long dominated the list of top finishers in New York, including a remarkable seven of the first nine male finishers in the 2003 race.

Many African-American basketball players from the inner cities of the United States see the NBA as one of the most attractive careers imaginable and are validated by the fact that more than three-quarters of the league is populated by African-Americans. Competition in that particular subculture of America is fierce, and top performers are celebrated from preteen years all the way to the culmination of their careers. The fact that more traditional career avenues are beset with numerous roadblocks only intensifies the natural selection process of developing the best basketball players. Similar cultural dynamics are in place in many other sports, such as the PGA Tour, where most had access to elitist private country clubs and a circuit of junior and collegiate tournaments to hone their competitive skills.

Human performance physician and cycling coach Max Testa of Intermountain Health Care in Salt Lake City may have summed up the nature versus nurture question best when he said, "Genes determine who makes it into the professional peloton [the French term to describe the pack of cyclists in a race], but not who wins the race." Testa is an authority on the popular VO_2 max laboratory performance test for endurance athletes. The test measures how efficiently an athlete utilizes oxygen during sustained strenuous exercise, expressed in milliliters of oxygen processed per kilogram of body weight. The resulting VO_2 max number is believed to have a direct application to the ultimate performance potential of an endurance athlete. Those with a high VO_2 max have the potential to reach elite performance level, while those without should alter their dreams. Testa explains, "VO_2 max is a combination of both genetic makeup and training effect. However, *trainability* [one's ability to improve VO_2 max through training] also has a strong genetic contribution."

The X Factor

There is another winning quality that is visible to the naked eye but more difficult to quantify or understand. The late author George Plimpton, famous for his works of participatory journalism such as *Paper Lion*, called it the "X Factor" in a book of the same name. Others use terms like *heart* or *character*, or as Bart Knaggs said to describe Lance's X Factor, "Lots of guys *want* to win; Lance *has* to win." The X Factor also looms large when you consider how many great talents there are in the pro ranks and how few stand out as legends. Bob Babbitt, publisher of *Competitor* magazine and long one of the most prominent journalists in the world of endurance sports, who has covered Lance's career for nearly two decades, adds, "I don't think Lance looked at his rivals as people, just objects. Like pieces of debris lying in the road. He might think they are nice guys that he could socialize with someday, but they were nevertheless in the way of something that he wanted. Certain people just have this killer instinct naturally."

"LOTS OF GUYS *WANT* TO WIN; LANCE *HAS* TO WIN."

—Bart Knaggs

What is the nature of this competitive flame that burns brightly inside some and is never lit in others? Why is it distributed seemingly randomly? Why is one sibling an intense and highly decorated competitor, while another is content to enjoy the view from the bleachers? Why are many kids with supportive and doting parents, year-round practice schedules, private conditioning coaches, and the latest $150 performance footwear never able to become truly inspired or skilled enough to make the varsity squad or carry on after high school? And how is some kid from a broken home clad in a rock star vest and ratty sneakers able to pick up a ball and throw a touchdown pass or outrun everyone else across the field with ease?

I asked Lance if he believed he was a born leader or destined to become a champion athlete. "I think 'born that way' is a little too easy of an answer," he responded. "There are probably some social issues—whatever's happened to you in life forces you to be a certain way. The way you're brought up, the values your parents gave you, or the examples they set mold you into a certain type of person—athlete, executive, whatever. Even in Little League—there's always a kid that's the leader of the team . . . uh, but that wasn't really me!"

In the business world the question becomes even more confusing. Like the athletes, you need good genes (for intelligence, in this case) to proceed with a quality education and eventually compete economically against the similarly endowed. Cultural influence is obviously huge, as proved by the widespread success enjoyed by certain cultural or ethnic groups that emphasize education or by graduates of elite universities. We know that a strong work ethic and people skills are important to end up in the CEO's chair or with advanced degrees and professional careers. However, talent and intelligence are frittered away in many directions—corporate politics or personal frailties like addiction, social disorders, ADD behavior, or simply a lack of ambition to pursue one's potential. On the flip side, there are numerous examples of those who come up short on brains, birth privilege, and connections but rise to the top, their dogged X Factor determination winning out over the bright and well positioned.

One of the most wonderful elements of competing in sports is how you learn the lessons of character and life in a graphic and dramatic manner. When you are well prepared, focused, and performing at your peak, you receive direct feedback in the competitive arena. There are no corporate politics to muddle up the distinction of top performers, nor can you turn to excuses, slick stories, and

TALENT SHOW AT THE FINISH LINE

*T*alent is a funny and often misused word in the athletic world. It has even found its way into politically incorrect and racist characterizations such as assertions that black basketball players are naturally quick and jump high while white basketball players shoot and pass well—a result of hard work on technique and strategic skills.

The best definition of talent relating to athletics I've heard came from Glenn Gaesser, professor of exercise physiology at the University of Virginia. During a lecture to athletes many years ago detailing VO_2 max test implications and other science-oriented topics, someone asked how to identify the most talented athletes. He paused dramatically to allow everyone to poise their pens, and then he said, "Go to a race and stand at the finish line. Then . . . see who crosses the line first. There is the most talented athlete." If you look at talent in this light instead of the usual talent versus hard work paradigm, a new possibility emerges: talent can take on a broader definition so that the ability to apply the focus, discipline, and motivation to put in hard work day after day, year after year becomes a highly esteemed type of talent. Particularly if you have great genetic abilities or have enjoyed the level of success that Lance Armstrong has, the potential for distraction is enormous.

My dad's characterization of professional athletes is accurate, but a truly freakish athletic talent is someone like Lance Armstrong with the whole package. Lance's body took to elite-level endurance training at a young age, and he has an extremely high VO_2 max value, an awesome work ethic, and one of the biggest X Factors ever witnessed in the history of sports. In his career, he had a string of good fortune with mentors and teammates, keeping away from trouble, injuries, and distractions. All of these factors had to fall into place for him to become the dominant professional athlete that he became.

devious positioning to make yourself look good when you can't cut it. The millions that professional teams spend on research, scouts, therapists, character analysis tests, and the like in attempts to protect and confirm their expensive human investments often tragically go to waste when athletes become diverted by the trappings of wealth, fame, or an undisciplined character.

Beyond the Hype

When subjected to the harmful influences of modern culture, such as the glorification of victory and violence in sports and the sensationalized hero worship of athletes, it's easy to get confused by the melodramatic, high-shock-value sound bites served up by the media. Instead of receiving inspiration and character lessons from great athletic performances, we become fixated on the hype. When we see an African runner excel, we conjure the fantasy of a small child running five miles barefoot each way to school daily through adulthood. It's not that simple. As 800-meter world-record holder Wilson Kipketer (a Kenyan who now represents Denmark in international competition) says, "I lived right next door to school. I walked, nice and slow." Perhaps part of our penchant for hyperbole and fantasy is to protect the ego from the reality that champion athletes work harder and are more deserving of glory than the average Joe off the street.

Athletes today are conditioned strongly to appreciate victory but not the enjoyment of the experience and striving to get better. With the young athletes I work with, it's surprising to observe the barrage of self-limiting statements and beliefs that they harbor about competition. At a recent practice session with high school high jumpers, one of the athletes announced to his peers, "I'm like the worst high jumper ever," just before launching himself at the bar. Second-grade children assembled for the distance race will whine, "Do I have to do it? I stink at running." The passenger next to me on a recent airplane flight told me she worked in a dental office but was "just an assistant," implying that this was not as valuable or impressive as being a dentist or certified hygienist. These self-deprecating comments that are ubiquitous today are simply a protection mechanism against the way we measure and judge everyone by their accomplishments. We worship money, victory, and prestige, while ignoring the subtler traits of exhibiting good sportsmanship, contributing goodwill to the community, or being a good listener, a mentor to youth or workplace associates, or generally a kind, decent, and fair person.

In my college economics class, we learned an interesting theory about how people are valued and compensated in an economy. The premise was advanced that everyone in a workplace is equally *valuable* and that compensation is determined by how *replaceable* they are. Theoretically, if a single person is missing from an assembly line, the product will not get made. If a computer server malfunctions in the workplace and the IT guy is out sick, the entire office is screwed. However, you can quickly train and insert a replacement to keep the line going or get the server operating.

Not so if the CEO decides to leave. Here you must embark upon a careful selection process to discover someone with the requisite skills and experience to run the show. Therefore, that person is compensated higher. This replaceability concept is the reason Jim Carrey can pull $20 million for a movie or Lance could command his millions for pedaling a bike. Imagine—*Help Wanted: accomplished cyclist to win the Tour de France, endorse products, and make personal appearances. Excellent salary and benefits package, extensive winter vacation time, and tons of free clothes and equipment. Send résumé to CSE, PO Box . . .*

We need to understand that there is way more to competition and achievement than the basic elements that are glamorized. Otherwise we will just sit around and watch those with the most raw talent and competitive instinct—the least replaceable performers—prevail, which is basically the essence of the fanaticism that surrounds professional sports. Millions more prefer to watch a basketball game on TV than to head down to the gym and participate in one.

In a high jump competition, the bar is set individually for each jumper, providing a completely personal challenge with unlimited potential for success. Everyone on the team has a chance to be a winner because everyone is capable of improving the height that they can clear. The metaphor of the high jump bar applies to whatever challenges and goals you have in your life. If your bar is set at becoming the best dental assistant you can be, there is great honor in that pursuit—far more honor than with a dentist who is more interested in deep-sea fishing than dentistry and just goes through the motions with the patients in his chair. As I explained to the young jumper after his statement, the "worst high jumper ever" is someone whose feet never leave the ground.

Twenty-Seven Hours

TV, magazine, and newspaper stories attempting to explain Lance's success invariably mention how his heart is 33 percent larger than the average man's and pumps so many extra liters of blood per minute. So what? The same is true for the other few hundred pro cyclists on the circuit who pedal six hundred miles each week. Daniel Coyle's *Lance Armstrong's War* details a simple performance test Lance did frequently throughout his career to gauge his fitness level. Conducted by Lance's trainer and noted cycling physician Dr. Michele Ferrari, the test measures the amount of lactic acid accumulated in the bloodstream in conjunction with watts of energy produced while cycling at high intensity. Dividing a rider's body weight by the number of watts he can sustain without "blowing up" (succumbing to lactic acid accumulation in the muscles) produces a value that Dr. Ferrari believes is a critical performance indicator. According to Dr. Ferrari, 6.7 watts per kilogram of body weight is the magic number that a rider must attain as a prerequisite for winning the Tour de France.

In Coyle's book Ferrari comments that Lance has a "natural" (as in predominantly genetic) advantage over his competition in the neighborhood of 2 percent because his muscles simply produce less acid waste product when hammering up a mountain than the next guy. However, Ferrari reminds us, this edge is not enough to account for seven dominant Tour de France victories.

Another recurring theme, "Lance trains harder than any other cyclist in the world," in and of itself means little. The guy who studied harder and longer than anyone in my freshman dorm nevertheless struggled with his grades. Once I glanced at one of his textbooks and noticed highlighter pen blanketing nearly every word on the pages!

What's more significant than Lance's "genetically gifted," "most competitive," and "hardest worker" yearbook nominations is how Lance was able to get the most out of his mind and body, avoid the burnout and overtraining that afflicts many top athletes, and peak at the exact right time for so many consecutive years. Being Lance's longtime friend, training partner, and business manager, Knaggs provides perhaps the most astute insights of anyone into Lance's peak performance attributes. Knaggs explains that the speed of Lance's brain is right up there with his pedaling speed as a key component of his winning formula.

"Like the flickering images that make up the display on a computer screen, our brains have a cognitive refresh rate," said Knaggs. "We take stock of our environment, recognize patterns, and make instantaneous assessments that govern our actions. This happens on a subconscious level. Lance's refresh rate is three times as fast as the average person's. He never zones out at any time; he's always hypervigilant, during the Tour and during his busy, multifaceted life. He's a good full step ahead of everybody, always thinking toward something, moving at a faster speed and never resting. He gets three hours out of the day that no one else does. At the end of the day, that mentality and that attitude do not allow him to accept anything less than absolute top effort from everyone around him."

"HE GETS THREE HOURS OUT OF THE DAY THAT NO ONE ELSE DOES."

—Bart Knaggs

Knaggs continues, "In this way, success is compounded by the little things that he does and how they rub off on people around him. Lance is always networking, finding the best people, being a shrewd assessor of talent, getting the best out of people, getting rid of people who don't work, finding better ones to replace them. On the other hand, people who come up short in one area or another, who zone out instead of remain focused, find that they compound failure. We have seen this with many of Lance's competitors. If you zone out for one second in a bike race, due to fatigue or whatever, you are at risk of a devastating crash.

"The reason Lance was so great at cycling is the complexity of the sport and the depth of the preparation required. Sure he has the boxer's mentality, which is important. But that alone will just get you overtrained or defeated in competition by a superior strategist. There are lots of athletes in that category. You also have to be smart. You have to be willing and motivated to do the right work, confident so you don't do too much or too little, and strategically prepared for a peak performance. You must never lack motivation, and you must have a strong desire to just eat people up—physically and mentally," Knaggs concludes.

Entering the Zone . . . with a Detour to the Bagel Shop

When I was a professional triathlete, I discovered that the mechanics of being an athlete were the simple part—turning the pedals, swimming the laps, and running the trails were fun, beat a real job, and got me in great shape. But the complex part that separated the winners from the rest of the pack went beyond cultural and genetic background and even work ethic.

A few years into my career, I realized that there was not much more physical effort I could apply to training and get better. In fact, my body was starting to rebel at the amount of physical stress placed on it, and I was frequently getting tired, burned out, and beaten by superior athletes on the racecourse. I realized that I needed to look in other directions for improvement, such as my lifestyle, beliefs, attitude, and behavior that affected performance.

I discovered that I needed to sacrifice personal diversions in favor of sleep, so I slept virtually half my life (ten hours per night with a one- to two-hour afternoon nap several days per week) to absorb the difficult training regimen that I followed for nine years. When I experienced disappointment on the racecourse, I had to learn to avoid the traps of negativity, defensiveness, and blame that we use as protective mechanisms when we don't get what we want. Falling prey to emotional and mental frailties just dug me into a deeper hole. Instead, I had to develop the ability to get out of bed the next morning with a positive attitude and high motivation levels intact. When faced with the intense pressure of a major competition, I had to develop the ability to remain calm, relaxed, and focused on personal peak performance.

My favorite line to describe this optimal approach is "Results happen naturally when motivation is pure." With a pure motivation, I would experience a higher level of performance without having to struggle or force anything. At those times, I was experiencing what James Loehr calls the "Ideal Performance State" (IPS), affectionately known as the zone. Loehr describes IPS in his book *Stress for Success* as "physically relaxed, mentally calm, fearless, energized, positive, happy, effortless, automatic, confident," and so on. We can all relate to times when we were in the zone and enjoyed breakthrough competitive performances—in athletic or other arenas. The hard part is staying in the zone for a sustained period of time and avoiding the distractions and pitfalls that come as a consequence of both failure and success. In contrast, being in the zone and embodying the clinical characteristics of the Ideal Performance State seem to be second nature to Lance.

At the 1988 Vancouver International Triathlon, local families housed the many professional athletes who flew in for this high-profile event. Lance (in the midst of his teenage foray onto the pro triathlon circuit) and I were staying in the same neighborhood near the race start and made plans to bicycle to the starting line on race morning. I appeared at his homestay at the appointed time; he was running well behind schedule. I waited impatiently, growing nervous that the already stressful prerace minutes were ticking off with an unplanned delay.

BEING IN THE ZONE AND EMBODYING THE CLINICAL CHARACTERISTICS OF THE IDEAL PERFORMANCE STATE SEEM TO BE SECOND NATURE TO LANCE.

Pedaling toward the waterfront race venue, we approached a bustling coffee and bagel shop, causing Lance to proclaim, "Man, I'm hungry. Let's stop for a bagel, B.K." While eating a bagel was the last thing on my mind (most athletes set their alarms for two or three hours before an event, consume some high-tech nutritional supplement like a liquid meal replacement or energy bar, and then go back to sleep), I indulged him in another detour. Circular snack in hand, Lance and I pedaled on toward the race venue, now dangerously close to the start time. While my nervousness and anxiety were building inside, I could not help but laugh at the sight of my riding partner rolling into the transition area with a bagel stuffed in his mouth.

As I completed my hurried prerace preparations and hustled off anxiously toward the start of the swim, I heard Lance yell, "Hey, B.K.!" As I turned to face him, he flashed the thumbs-up sign and said, "Let's kick some ass today!" Instantly, my nervousness and tension melted away into a big smile, thanks to a fellow competitor no less. On the short walk to the swim start, I could feel my anxious state being transformed into the Ideal Performance State. I realized that the great pains athletes take to be prepared, follow their obsessive but comforting precompetition rituals, account for all variables, and show up on time pale in comparison to having a kick-ass mindset. After all, we were there to race our brains out for two hours, not for a job interview.

Don't get me wrong. Being serious and professional in your approach is critical. The teenage, bagel-scarfing Lance arriving at the race at the last minute is a far cry from the Tour de France champion noted for his tremendous attention to detail and devoted preparation. However, I'll always bet on someone who shows up late ready to win over someone with all their ducks lined up neatly but feeling insecure and fearful about the competition.

Athletes and other performers express their precompetition jitters in different ways. Some turn inward and suffer anxiety solemnly, some play the macho intimidator role to artificially boost confidence, and others engage in serial self-deprecating comments or become insincerely friendly and chatty. These "game face" acts can create negative energy because they all suggest a doomed attempt to fight against and somehow overcome the butterflies that are a natural and healthy component of the body's stress response.

If, instead, you were able to go with the flow, be honest with yourself, and be completely positive in the face of an important competition, you would then be able to enter the zone effortlessly. Consider this passage from Martin Dugard (author of *Chasing Lance: The 2005 Tour de France and Lance Armstrong's Ride of a Lifetime*), which appeared in a September 2001 article in *Competitor* magazine (reprinted by permission). Dugard comments about Lance's disposition in the final days of the 2001 Tour, as he witnessed this scene unfold in a small French restaurant:

A lean young man descended the staircase above my head, displaying the charisma and presence of a Kennedy, then rushed into the arms of a child screaming, "Daddy-yo-yo." The restaurant staff looked as if they were barely restraining themselves to do the same.

For the next half-hour, Lance (does anyone refer to him as "Armstrong" anymore?) played with his son, made nice with the folks from Nike and U.S. Postal Service, and lamented to his wife that they were sleeping in separate rooms again. He sounded like any other husband during a dry spell, which made him come across as human. Which was refreshing, because Lance's relaxation was almost inhuman.

At that moment, he was leading the Tour de France, just three days from winning his third consecutive title. The next morning, Lance would face a make-or-break individual time trial, 61 kilometers against the clock with no one to blame but himself for a bad day. The Tour was far from done. Losing the lead in the last week would make "Lance" a household name for failure instead of heroism.

Not that Lance seemed to care. Where he should have been nervous, he was joking. Where he should have been distant and forgivingly brusque, he worked the table like a pro before disappearing back upstairs, son in tow, so his wife could eat dinner in peace.

Lance was not only destroying the Tour field, he was giving weekend warrior husbands a bad name. The "I've got a race tomorrow" excuse just became very, very lame.

At the risk of sounding abrasive, athletes or those otherwise consumed with a peak performance endeavor deserve to read this passage over a few times. (Or, if you play the role of supportive partner, read this section aloud to your partner!) It seems paradoxical that Lance, facing the most extreme pressure imaginable in world-level

"THE 'I'VE GOT A RACE TOMORROW' EXCUSE JUST BECAME VERY, VERY LAME."

—Martin Dugard

competition, can be looser and more relaxed than the average tightly strung amateur competitor in a local triathlon. Like many paradoxes, therein lies an important secret to achieving peak performance breakthroughs: get over yourself and the negative nervous energy generated by an obsession with results. Instead, just go out there and kick some ass today!

Graham Watson, grahamwatson.com

3

THE SUCCESS FACTORS IN ACTION

The fact that Lance was able to win the Tour de France seven times in a row in modern times is an extraordinary phenomenon. While there is much debate about the merits of comparing athletes from different time periods, one thing is certain: the explosion in popularity of professional sports has enabled the powerful forces of the free market to escalate the competition to levels far exceeding that of a generation or even a decade ago.

Dominant athletes have been around forever, but the superstars of yesterday had the advantages of a tilted playing field. When Eddy Merckx ruled the sport of cycling in the 1960s and '70s, he was competing against a talent pool limited to western European countries. The financial incentive to be an average professional cyclist was minimal, further discouraging widespread talent development and healthy competition in that "marketplace."

Until the past couple decades, most potential champion athletes had to concern themselves with making a living after their school days ended. Many of the best athletes were lost to the ranks of coal miners, factory workers, and even business professionals. Consider Sir Roger Bannister of England, the first man to run a four-minute mile, who retired in his prime at age twenty-five to pursue a career as a physician. In contrast, the 2006 retirement of mile-world-record holder Hicham El Guerrouj at age thirty-one was truly a retirement; the Moroccan left sports a very wealthy man and a national hero to boot. Economic incentives in high-level sports are a powerful consequence to the fact that El Guerrouj's mile record today (2006) stands at three minutes, forty-three seconds. In Bannister's time, many considered the four-minute mile the ultimate limitation of human potential.

It's been widely reported that Lance, at the tail end of his career, earned in the neighborhood of $18 million a year in salary and endorsements by virtue of his cycling performances. The exorbitant wealth and worldwide exposure that the Tour de France champion receives has created an efficient natural selection process to discover and develop the finest cycling talent across the globe.

When a special talent is discovered, enormous resources—including coaching, equipment, training regimens, competitive environments, technique instruction, and mental training—are committed to develop him into a champion. These resources are both state supported, such as the famed East German sports machine of the 1970s and '80s that handpicked the most promising athletes in grade school and sent them away to special sports schools to develop them into Olympians, and driven by private enterprise, such as the cases of teenage skateboarding phenoms landing endorsement contracts (ensuring their path to the top is not distracted by trivial matters like school or work).

With Lance growing up in Texas, he first had to discover a lack of interest and aptitude in the default cultural favorite of football to drift to more suitable sports of swimming and distance running. When the IronKids national series of minitriathlons came to town and Lance prevailed all the way to being the national age-group champion, the wheels were in motion to his ultimate destination. People and resources started popping up in his life to assist him on the road to excellence in his area of natural talent.

By high school, Lance was earning extra pocket money (as in $20,000-plus a year) racing on the pro triathlon circuit. However, like many young American athletes in their relevant sports, the Olympics were his driving ambition. Soon he left home and his part-time triathlon job to train with the U.S. National Junior Cycling team in Colorado. He signed with the Subaru-Montgomery team (earning a modest salary yet retaining his amateur, Olympic status under the quirky rules of the days before full professionalism), competed in the 1992 Olympics (after which he officially turned pro), and then hit the big time with his 1993 World Championships win.

While some potential champions do slip through the cracks for personal reasons and lack of adequate support systems, it doesn't happen very often. *C'est impossible* to validate some Frenchman working on a road-paving crew, lamenting that he could have defeated Armstrong but for lack of funds to afford a proper racing bike or time off work to train.

Many athletes in the professional ranks have stories similar to Lance's—they showed a talent and affinity for a certain sport as youths and were developed through local, national, and professional infrastructures that exist across the globe. As a consequence of this international free-market operation with minimal entry barriers, we see people from the most diverse and unlikely backgrounds congregating on the starting line. Athletes in the 2005 Tour de France represented twenty-eight nations, including unlikely locations like Ukraine, Kazakhstan, Uzbekistan, and Slovenia, as well as everything from affluent urban centers across Europe and the Americas to small backcountry farm towns.

This sports selection process is applied to millions, beginning in childhood and escalating in intensity as the level of competition and incentives rise. Athletes who make the big time (the Olympics, Major League Baseball, the National Basketball Association, the National Football League, the National Hockey League, the PGA

Tour, and so on) today are a group of supertalents performing at a similar level on the cutting edge of human potential—a "parity of excellence" condition in modern sport. On occasion, we see human statistical aberrations like Lance Armstrong (and Tiger Woods, Annika Sorenstam, Hicham El Guerrouj, and others) rise above the parity of excellence to dominate against astronomical odds. Lance's constant superiority over his rivals during his seven-year run anesthetized us to the difficulty of winning the Tour de France, let alone winning repeatedly. "Wait until the mountains and the time trials— Lance will take a couple minutes out of his rivals and win the yellow jersey," went the mainstream sports fan's keen insight.

Sure enough, time and time again Lance did just that to our great appreciation. But it's impossible to truly appreciate what took place unless you were to pedal your bike in the Tour de France peloton for five hours over mountainous terrain at high intensity, accumulating unimaginable fatigue in every muscle in your body. Then, upon reaching the foot of a massive climb to the finish line, you must ascend it at 100 percent effort to break away from a pack of the greatest cyclists in the world. This is where Lance "easily" took a couple minutes out of his rivals every year. Then he got back on his bike the following day for more of the same!

Killer Instinct

It's fascinating to match the mind-sets and quotes of athletes with their performances. At the inaugural Olympic triathlon competition in Sydney, Australia, in 2000, Canadian Simon Whitfield achieved a remarkable victory. Behind late in the run (the final event) by a seemingly insurmountable distance, he exploded over the final 400 meters to somehow catch the front-running German Stefan Vuckovic just meters before the finish line. After the race, Vuckovic explained that his goal was to win a medal—he didn't care what color. With a substantial lead nearing the finish, Vuckovic looked back numerous times, likely to ensure that a pack was not converging to knock him out of medal position. As Whitfield blew by him, Vuckovic continued his pace, celebrating on a par with Simon in the finishing stretch en route to his silver medal. Whitfield's postrace comment was that he gave 100 percent effort to the very end, never losing the belief that a gold medal was possible.

LANCE'S CONSTANT SUPERIORITY OVER HIS RIVALS DURING HIS SEVEN-YEAR RUN ANESTHETIZED US TO THE DIFFICULTY OF WINNING THE TOUR DE FRANCE, LET ALONE WINNING REPEATEDLY.

To be respectful of great athletes like Vuckovic (who has admirably overcome serious health problems to compete as a top professional) or those that Lance has left in his wake on the roads of the Tour de France, we should note that everyone in the professional ranks is a great competitor with a tremendous winning instinct. However, when the stakes escalate and an athlete has to tap into his deepest reserves to pursue victory, the difference between a tough competitor and an absolutely ferocious one who will win or die clearly reveals itself.

"Certain athletes accept nothing less than victory," explains Martin Dugard, who has a unique author pedigree, having written books on such divergent subjects as endurance races like the Tour de France and the Raid Gauloises to historical accounts of great explorers like Columbus and Captain Cook. At the four Tour de France events he covered, Dugard saw firsthand the tremendous power and intensity of Lance's clear purpose to win the Tour de France. "Throughout the Tour, Lance remained totally focused on the moment and on his ultimate goal—no matter what. Most of the other athletes reach a point where they are just trying to hold on. They find their mind wandering and their resolve weakening as they suffer from the accumulated pain of intense effort for three weeks."

Someone who is out for blood can smell these nuances and viciously attack them. "Up close, it's apparent that Lance is an absolutely ferocious competitor," continues Dugard. "He is committed to winning and making sure that everyone remembers it! At the same time, he is diplomatic to the media and exhibits impeccable sportsmanship on the racecourse. This is what the public demands; we want to see athletic domination, but we don't like it when people go overboard.

"I think the reason for this may have to do with our evolution to a relatively more civilized modern world," Dugard continues. "Throughout history, mankind has embraced conflict, domination over opponents, and doing whatever it takes to achieve victory. It's part of our basic human nature to want to push things to the extreme and conquer our environment. These elements of our nature have been the root cause of war throughout the centuries. As society has evolved to appreciate the value of world peace, we seem to want to suppress that element of humanity in the name of getting along," concludes Dugard.

It's clear from today's epidemic of poor sportsmanship at all levels of work and play, and the hero worship and fanaticism surrounding big-time (and even small-time) sports, that society still worships victory at all costs. Conversely, many have successfully suppressed any latent competitive instincts and thus have little to show in the peak performance category. Both sides of the coin are troubling and cause us to have difficulty taking the risks required for peak performance, competing with full passion and intensity and developing pure confidence in our abilities. There is so much at stake that we feel incredible pressure to perform and measure up to the "winner or loser" judgments placed upon us by society and also to not act like an ass in the process.

Dory O You?

In Japanese sports and corporate culture, an important core value is expressed by the concept of *doryoku*, which means a visible demonstration of hard work and giving one's best, where commitment and effort are rewarded over achievement. In Robert Whiting's *You Gotta Have Wa*, an entertaining inside look at the wildly popular professional baseball league in Japan, a recurring theme is the conflict that imported American baseball stars have with the Japanese system's emphasis on *doryoku*. Japanese teams push their players through marathon practices, even in the steamy heat of a Japanese summer. Pitchers throw hundreds of pitches daily, instead of the more familiar and sensible rotation of effort practiced by American throwers. To Japanese players, their heavy workload is expected in the spirit of *doryoku*, while the Americans bristle and rebel over what they think is ridiculous overkill.

Considering the Japanese won the first-ever World Baseball Classic (in 2006), it may make sense to drift a little closer in the direction of *doryoku* and away from the "me first, win or else" elements of American culture. Lance's unwavering focus in training and love of all elements of the cycling lifestyle—his *doryoku*—enabled him to become a very powerful conqueror. By emphasizing commitment and effort, he enjoyed a consequent windfall of positive results. There are plenty of similar examples from all walks of life, like the Stanford computer science doctoral students Larry Page and Sergey Brin, who became consumed with building a better search engine. They withdrew from school and founded a small company in a friend's garage in Palo Alto, California. They kept their heads down while their counterparts in the Silicon Valley were cashing big checks from initial public offerings. With their restraint, long-term focus, and commitment to innovation, they woke up one day a few years later as Prius-driving, socially conscious Google billionaires.

Everyone from big-time athletes to those competing to survive the trials and tribulations of daily life must reflect on their level of

---

LANCE'S UNWAVERING FOCUS IN TRAINING AND LOVE OF ALL ELEMENTS OF THE CYCLING LIFESTYLE—HIS *DORYOKU*—ENABLED HIM TO BECOME A VERY POWERFUL CONQUEROR.

---

doryoku, understanding that it can unlock the most enlightened and enjoyable path to success. *Lose weight now, ask me how?* OK, get off your can and start exercising your body. Take decisive action to eat healthy, natural foods instead of succumbing to the corporate-driven momentum to consume the processed toxic crap of the modern American diet. Make some effort and commitment to do these things so that you can enjoy your life more. Consequently, you will lose weight—sorry, not "now," but gradually and maybe permanently. Want to *get rich quick*? That's easy—pause, take a deep breath, look around you, and count your simple blessings of health, family, friends, and community.

Lance Lessons for Business

There is a strong parallel between the athletic arena and the business world, where competitive success is clearly measured by the real-life element of money. It's no wonder that corporate lingo and slogans are littered ad nauseam with sports metaphors. Tim Bauman, a former executive at the business information systems corporation Unisys, handed out footballs to reward employee accomplishments. Neither he nor virtually any other male and female on his team ever played organized tackle football, but everyone appreciates the symbolism of this game ball, locker-room tradition.

Martin Brauns, former CEO of Interwoven, has enjoyed a unique viewpoint to see the power of Lance's example as applied to the business world. Brauns first met Lance in 2000, when he hired Lance to speak at the firm's first-ever worldwide user conference in San Francisco, and his initial impression was powerful. "Immediately it was apparent the intensity and focus of this man— just from the way he looked at me. He showed a tremendous amount of class stepping up onto a stage in front of a thousand people and giving a great speech. After all, he was probably a bit disappointed only a couple days removed from the Olympics [Lance won a bronze medal in the time trial in Sydney after being favored to win]."

It's worth noting that the observer in this case is a far cry from the moneyed sycophants who hover around our sports heroes, buying teams, collecting expensive memorabilia, or paying five figures to spend a weekend at fantasy camps. Brauns is a self-described "fiercely intense competitor" who assumed the CEO role at Interwoven at the ripe age of thirty-eight. He promptly led the software company to a successful initial public offering in 1999 (becoming independently wealthy before hitting forty) and to the distinction of being named in the November 2000 *Investor's Business Daily* as the world's fastest-growing technology company, with a three-year sales growth rate of 719 percent.

For a hobby, Brauns took up the consuming endeavor of triathlon. A year after starting the sport, he completed the most grueling triathlon competition on earth, the Ultraman, on the big island of Hawaii—a ramp up in racing distance unprecedented in the history of triathlon. The Ultraman makes the more popular Ironman seem like a warm-up. The three-day competition consists of a 6.2-mile swim and 90-mile bike ride on day one, a 171-mile bike ride (completing a circumnavigation of the island) on day two, and, finally, a 52.4-mile double marathon run in the steamy, inhospitable conditions of the Kona lava fields on day three.

Unbeknownst to Brauns (until he reads this book), Lance enthusiastically remarked to me later in the day they first met, "Wow that guy [Brauns] is intense!" The two peas in a pod hit it off quickly, and Bill Stapleton cemented a four-year sponsorship agreement the following day. While Brauns makes a point of disqualifying himself from being a Lance insider or even knowing him beyond a basic professional relationship, he offers keen insights about the beauty of the Lance operation from a corporate perspective.

"It's obvious the discipline and focus Lance applied to win the Tour de France and to beat cancer," Brauns remarks. "That single-minded focus and intensity is, of course, extremely applicable to the business world. The first question a business or an athlete should ask is, 'What do you want to do? What hill do you want to climb?' Businesses have to pursue the right market. When venture-capital firms decide where to invest their money, they don't think just in terms of 'Can we dominate in this market?' More important, they decide whether they *want* to dominate a particular market. It's no big deal to muscle into some tiny market and dominate."

Brauns continues, "Once focused on a business goal, the next step is to assemble a top-notch team—a leader, a board of directors, an executive team, sales staff, audit and legal advisers, etc. Lance has obviously taken a far more active role at this than any other rider and done this better than anyone. Besides hiring a good team, it's important to compensate them well and give them credit."

In Lance's interviews and podium speeches, he was forever mentioning the strength of his team and lavishing praise on them. Due to the scope of his undertaking, his team included not only the riders in uniform but team director Johan Bruyneel (Lance's chief strategist for all seven victories) and the large support staff (bike mechanics, massage therapists, cooks, logistics coordinators, health care practitioners, and so on), his coach Chris Carmichael, trainer and performance physician Dr. Michele Ferrari, and his business and personal affairs management team of Bart Knaggs,

Bill Stapleton, and the rest of the staff at Capital Sports and Entertainment.

HE WAS FOREVER MENTIONING THE STRENGTH OF HIS TEAM AND LAVISHING PRAISE ON THEM.

Cycling tradition has it that a winning rider shares his purse with the team, so the nearly $500,000 that goes to the yellow jersey winner in the Tour de France was divvied up among his teammates. Furthermore, Lance reached into his pocket every year to bestow an additional mid-five-figure bonus on the other eight riders that make up his Tour de France team.

Lance skillfully leveraged his penchant for generosity. Take the case of American Floyd Landis, whose 2006 Tour de France victory was spoiled by a doping violation, as related in Lance's book *Every Second Counts*. Landis was handpicked by Lance from the obscure American circuit and mentored into becoming one of the finest cyclists in the world. Soon after Landis joined the U.S. Postal Service squad in 2001, Lance sensed that Landis's commitment was wavering, in part due to the financial stress of supporting a young marriage on the moderate earnings of a pro cyclist. Lance explained to Landis that if he were to be selected for the Tour de France roster (a team like the U.S. Postal Service carried a couple dozen riders on the roster, while only the fittest nine are selected for the Tour), he could likely earn victory bonuses that would essentially triple his annual compensation. In the process, he would alleviate financial pressure and ensure the continued advancement of his career and compensation. The alternative, as is the case for many fine athletes in secondary sports who are on the performance margin, is a quick ticket out of sports and onto a forklift, moving pallets around a warehouse.

Landis was inspired to lose weight (a sure sign of commitment, and often the difference between a marginal rider and a good one due to the tremendous influence on performance that even a couple pounds can make when climbing mountains) and intensify his training focus, which resulted in his earning a spot among the elite U.S. Postal nine. After a couple years of spectacular performances in the Tour in service of Lance, Landis became such a hot commodity that he left the team to lead another for a large salary, thereby becoming one of Lance's main rivals!

Tunnel Vision

"After assembling a great team," Brauns explains, "a business must employ *best practices*, a term to describe efficient components of a business entity like assembly lines, inventory management, shipping and receiving, order processing, and so on. A business will observe the competition to gain best practices insights, and then it will innovate to gain a competitive edge. When Lance and Johan Bruyneel first sat down in 1998 and devised a plan to win the 1999 Tour de France, they evaluated the best practices of other riders and teams and then developed a plan of action for Lance. After proving the success of their plan with successive victories, they developed what can be considered valuable intellectual property—Lance's training template for preparing and peaking for the Tour every July.

"Lance and his team also deployed *best technology* and used that technology appropriately to gain the most strategic leverage," Brauns adds. In the old-school world of European professional cycling, where superstitions abound and many leading teams, riders, and trainers subscribe to woefully outdated training strategies, dietary habits, and even competitive strategy, American innovations have turned the sport upside down at the expense of the traditionalists. The most dramatic example occurred in the 1989 Tour de France, where American Greg LeMond debuted the aerodynamic handlebars that have been recognized as the greatest cycling performance innovation of the past century. These ridiculous-looking bullhorn-shaped bars were scoffed at by the Europeans, but LeMond's more efficient riding position made the difference and then some in the eight-second victory he gained over Frenchman Laurent Fignon, the closest finish in Tour history.

Entire documentaries have aired on the cable outlets Outdoor Life Network and Discovery Channel revealing the tremendous scope of technology R&D for the equipment Lance used to win the Tour de France. Over the years, Lance regularly visited "wind tunnel" testing facilities, where computerized equipment measures the aerodynamic drag of a rider riding a stationary bike into airflow produced by a jet engine. Testing different bicycles, wheels, handlebars, and riding postures—even garments and helmets—helped Lance refine his setup and riding position to become ever more aerodynamic.

"THEY EVALUATED THE BEST PRACTICES OF OTHER RIDERS AND TEAMS AND THEN DEVELOPED A PLAN OF ACTION FOR LANCE."

—Martin Brauns

Note that aerodynamics is of little importance to riders in a pack along the relatively flat roads that make up most of the miles of the Tour. Riders at the front of the pack (a position that is constantly rotated into by fresh riders) create a slipstream for following riders, dramatically reducing their pedaling effort and minimizing the impact of the aerodynamic drag they produce on their performance. For example, crouching down lower makes little difference when riding in a slipstream of air created by a rider in front; doing so riding solo reduces effort and improves speed significantly. A team leader like Lance will be shielded from the wind by his teammates at all times on flat terrain of the Tour. When climbing mountains, wind resistance again becomes a minor factor due to the slow speeds (the relevance of wind resistance on performance rises and falls exponentially as you speed up or slow down) and the increased importance of raw muscular and cardiovascular power to tackle steep terrain.

In time trial competitions, aerodynamics is critical. These solo races against the clock are typically contested for three of the twenty-plus stages of the Tour. Riders are staggered by regular starting intervals, ride alone for the duration of the event, and each record a separate finishing time. This time is added to their cumulative time in the overall standings. A time trial is known as the "race of truth" because the fittest riders are clearly distinguished thanks to the elimination of strategy and the wind protection of a pack. Because of the high speeds attained and constant presence of the direct wind resistance during a time trial, even a slight improvement in aerodynamics (say, using a teardrop-shaped helmet or lowering your torso slightly) can shave a minute off a rider's finishing time in an hour time trial. In 2003 a minute was Lance's margin of victory over the entire three-week, 2,125-mile Tour de France.

Beyond the obsession with aerodynamics, Lance's team popularized the use of radio communications between team director and riders on the road, wattage meters to determine energy output while training, blood lactate testing to measure fitness progress, cutting-edge bicycle and component part technology, and even apparel designed to provide maximum cooling effect and minimal wind resistance. Did Lance gain a huge advantage over his competitors with his space-age breathable aerodynamic Nike racing suits or his top-of-the-line Trek bicycles? Not a chance. In my opinion, some of these high-tech R&D projects were merely feeding the consumerism machine that participatory amateur sports like cycling have become, where people will buy anything hip, slick, cool, and used by Lance.

However, the mentality that this comprehensive, methodical approach fostered with every single person involved with the team was a critical component in their success. Consider a rank-and-file rider who signs up for the U.S. Postal—later, Discovery Channel—team and notices the time, energy, and human resources devoted to ensuring that he eats the right breakfast every day and has a carefully prepared training program, physiological tests to track progress, and a bike designed to his exact specifications and presented to him daily, squeaky clean and in perfect working order. Do you think it improves his competitive mind-set a little, not to mention his self-esteem and devotion to the higher goal of getting Lance to the Tour de France finish line ahead of everyone? Do you think the sum total of the massive commitment to the concept of best technology by Lance and his team made for small advantages here and there over less attentive and progressive riders and teams? Absolutely. Furthermore, a competitor like Lance can take a small advantage and exploit it into a dominant performance.

A COMPETITOR LIKE LANCE CAN TAKE A SMALL ADVANTAGE AND EXPLOIT IT INTO A DOMINANT PERFORMANCE.

Compounded Interest

"Does technology matter?" Knaggs ponders. "Well, Lance almost lost the 2003 Tour, for a variety of reasons. Shortly before the Tour, he switched to a brand-new frame with stiffer crank arms, along with new pedals and cleats. Going with a completely new setup is something he would not ordinarily do. Normally it's a step-by-step progression to integrate new equipment. Why did he do it? I think he was a little lost before the 2003 Tour—a little confused, not as focused, not quite right with his fitness and mind-set. Close observers like Bruyneel and Carmichael also commented that he didn't seem to have that Lance magic, that 'it' that is the piercing stare, complete confidence, the zone of aggression and complete certainty where he feels like he can walk through a brick wall.

"It's funny how these little issues compound and create momentum," Knaggs continues. "The typical story in the Tour was: Lance gets to the first day of mountains, full of piss and vinegar, unleashes on everybody, cracks them mentally, and they start to roll over and play dead. Whether they realize it or not, he's in their heads. He owns them, and he spends the rest of the race just screwing with their heads. In 2003 it was different. He wanted to open a can of whup-ass on his rivals, but he couldn't. People stayed with him or even broke away. In that critical stage [over the Galibier and Alpe d'Huez, stage eight], he came on the radio and said to Johan and me [in the team support vehicle following Lance along the route], 'I have good news and bad news: my rear brake has been rubbing against my tire all day!'"

"I HAVE GOOD NEWS AND BAD NEWS: MY REAR BRAKE HAS BEEN RUBBING AGAINST MY TIRE ALL DAY!"

—Lance Armstrong

Knaggs continues, "In 2003 Lance had difficulties with his setup, the brakes rubbing, an illness before the event, the dehydration in the stage twelve time trial. He didn't have it but he got through the event with guts and moxie. He was in a title fight, getting taken to the late rounds and getting outpointed. He could have lost the fight, but instead, the crash on the climb to Luz Ardiden in stage fifteen woke him up, and he got angry and aggressive. He remembered that he was Lance Armstrong and that he crushes people on bikes and pulled it out.

"At the end of the day, the bike rider wins a bike race," Knaggs summarizes. "But his 2003 struggles [in contrast to other years] reveal what winning a three-week Tour is all about: it requires a hundred substantive decisions, with a thousand chances to make a dumb error or create your own bad luck in the three-week race—and in the two hundred fifty days of training to prepare for it. If you don't have 100 percent of the peripheral resources nailed, doubt and bad luck find a way to drift in."

> "IF YOU DON'T HAVE 100 PERCENT OF THE PERIPHERAL RESOURCES NAILED, DOUBT AND BAD LUCK FIND A WAY TO DRIFT IN."
>
> —Bart Knaggs

(Speed of) Sound Investments

"The team devoted time and energy to areas where they believed an advantage could be gained over the competition or was otherwise critical to their success," commented Brauns. Early in his career, Lance and the CSE boys made the decision to lease a share in a corporate jet, a shamefully expensive mode of travel (a *Sports Illustrated* article reported that a quick hop from Lance's home in Austin to Lincoln, Nebraska—to appear at a charity event with rock singer Bono—ran a cool fifteen grand) that an outsider might consider a frivolous luxury.

SUCCESS FACTORS AND LUCK

In the aforementioned 2003 Tour de France that was Lance's closest margin of victory, the outcome was still undecided on the final day of real racing, an individual time trial. Perennial bridesmaid Jan Ullrich was only one minute, five seconds behind and had beaten Lance by one minute, twenty-six seconds in the previous time trial (where Lance became dehydrated). In the latter part of the course, Ullrich crashed on a rainy traffic roundabout, ending his chances to overtake Lance. One journalist commented on the numerous occasions of bad luck suffered by a succession of those who dared to challenge Lance. Upon closer inspection, some facts were revealed that can draw us away from an explanation of "luck" and toward yet another shining example of Lance's application of success factors like specialized intelligence and pure confidence.

Lance previewed the course in training and also on the morning of the event, driving the route with Bruyneel in the pouring rain. Lance noticed that "the last 10 kilometers [6.2 miles] had lots of corners and lots of painting [less traction for bike tires] on the road. It was dangerous. I decided to start slowly and race at my own tempo. I was confident, knowing that with a minute lead over Jan, with the rain, the wind, and the dangerous course, I had no reason to take risks." On the other hand, Ullrich weathered the morning storm in his hotel, opting for his team manager to *videotape* the route for him. Stage winner and world time-trial champion David Millar of Great Britain said, "I saw Jan Ullrich in the first kilometer and said to myself, 'Man, he'll go down today!'"

If this example causes you to utter a sarcastic quip or is otherwise difficult to relate to, reflect for a moment on how this decision demonstrated Lance's priorities. To Lance, the ability to spend maximum time with his family and respect the importance of rest for an athlete by minimizing the stress of air travel was worth any financial sacrifice. Most of us are afraid or unwilling to make comparable commitments, but champions invest in themselves and their future, even when it may not seem financially sensible. When I extol the benefits of eating healthy foods, like choosing organic produce over conventional or favoring a market like Whole Foods over a mainstream grocery chain, the first comment I get from most is, "too expensive." Too expensive relative to what? Is there a better investment than your health?

CHAMPIONS INVEST IN THEMSELVES AND THEIR FUTURE, EVEN WHEN IT MAY NOT SEEM FINANCIALLY SENSIBLE.

Brauns's commentary from his lofty vantage point in the CEO chair is naturally different from the perspective shared by an individual contributor to the team. Someone in accounts payable jabbering about the big picture and losing focus on the little picture of his daily responsibilities is punching his ticket out the door. Even many top professional athletes do not have the vision that Lance has, as they are more inclined to focus on next week's game or the day's training session. However, we are all the CEOs of our own lives. We can take control of our health, our peak performance goals—athletic or otherwise—and what we bring to the table when we are part of something greater than ourselves, such as a company, our family, or another team structure.

Graham Watson, grahamwatson.com

4

SUCCESS FACTOR 1
POSITIVE ATTITUDE

t was a muggy spring afternoon in Austin at the 2001 Lance Armstrong Foundation's Ride for the Roses weekend. The annual event celebrates cancer survivors and foundation contributors with numerous festivities around town, like a gala awards banquet and a group bike ride with thousands of participants. As was his custom, Lance flew in from his European training base for a quick weekend of jam-packed appearances. One was an outdoor cocktail reception at the Four Seasons Hotel, where I took the opportunity to perform one of the more lecherous elements of my job—mooching autographs from Lance for various VIP designees connected to Interwoven.

I spread out a stack of posters, and Lance dove right in. His task was hindered by a succession of pretty aggressive sneezes (not on the posters though). His nose was red and his eyes a bit watery. As soon as he'd disembarked from his jet coming from Europe, he'd obviously fallen victim to allergies, which are notoriously bad that time of year in Texas. I, too, had struggled since arriving in Austin. The air seemed visibly heavy and dirty, and my runs along the beautiful Lake Austin trail downtown felt sluggish and hindered by constricted lungs.

I remarked to Lance, "I can't believe how bad the allergies are here! I don't see how you can even train, I mean . . ." At which point Lance paused his pen, looked me right in the eye, and said, "Quit bitching." I was a little taken aback; after all, this was a cocktail reception, and I was making small talk about the weather per cultural custom. For the moment, I passed it off as Lance just being Lance.

Upon further reflection, I realized that I had learned a valuable lesson. How dare I complain about the weather, to a cancer survivor, at a gathering of cancer survivors, in a beautiful town like Austin! Weather—and being outdoors to experience it—is a gift to be enjoyed and appreciated every day. Instead, we often adopt a negative attitude about weather, judging it to be too hot, too cold, or otherwise annoying and problematic. What's the big deal? Well, small talk and negative opinions and beliefs have a way of adding up to become big problems with our attitudes. Even a seemingly inconsequential subject like your attitude about the weather deserves to be challenged and reframed into something positive.

The Greatest Human Freedom

The most life-changing insight I have taken from Lance is his intense and unwavering positive attitude. The Lance Armstrong Foundation's "Live Strong" motto is about spreading hope and inspiration to the cancer community and adopting a positive attitude to face difficult circumstances—to live strong in the face of adversity. "It's critical to remain positive, whether it's at work, racing a bike, or fighting an illness," says Lance. "Everyone has different temperaments—some people are aggressive, some more relaxed, some more emotional. I think the important thing is to maintain a positive attitude, which can be fostered in many ways. Everyone walks and talks differently—you can have a relaxed, calm positive attitude or a very excitable, emotional positive attitude.

"In a life-or-death situation like my illness, I had no choice but to be positive," Lance continues. "I had to believe in my doctors, medicine, and treatment protocol and in myself that I could beat it. I wasn't cynical at all, wasn't skeptical—I was absolutely convinced that I was going to get better." I asked him if this was automatic or if it took some effort to adopt his positive attitude. "Well, my diagnosis [on October 2, 1996] was sudden, surprising, and quite serious. For a few days I was in shock—crying, scared, and feeling great despair. Then as I went about the process of doing my research, I saw a glimpse of hope. I found the best doctors and the best place to get treatment and realized the possibility of recovery. After that it was automatic.

"I prepared for my treatment like it was a bike race," Lance explains. "I made cancer like an opponent that I hated and wanted to beat very badly. I believe the athletic approach, the athletic mentality, was very beneficial. I did everything with 100 percent efficiency, just as you must do to peak for a championship race. My research, understanding the drugs and the treatment protocol, taking care of my body, eating a healthy diet—I went 100 percent on everything. Fortunately, I had graphic feedback during my treatment, and this helped me maintain a positive attitude. Every week I had a chest x-ray where I could see the lesions shrinking in front of my eyes. I had highly accurate blood work telling me that the cancer was going away. It was like riding a time trial and hearing on the radio that I am putting time on my opponents. Now winning a race feels good, but when you are dealing with life or death and you are getting good news—that is a real rush!"

According to Viktor Frankel, Holocaust survivor and author of the classic *Man's Search for Meaning*, "The greatest human freedom is the freedom to choose one's attitude." You always have the ability and the freedom to choose a positive attitude, no matter what your circumstances. It's hard to imagine a more difficult situation in which to retain a positive attitude than with Lance's shocking cancer diagnosis, but he was able to do it and gave himself no other choice. Lance's positive attitude created an environment around him that was influenced by this mind-set. Was this the reason he recovered from cancer? Not exactly, for many positive people succumb to illness and other misfortunes. And many negative, bitter people go through chemo and walk away cured. However, Lance's mindset helped him through his ordeal in a significant way, and science is having ever greater success connecting emotional states to immune function and healing.

When difficult circumstances and your ability to choose a positive attitude are severely tested and you pass the test, you strengthen your resolve to be positive in the future. Those who are not able to stay in control of their attitudes, who let the world beat them down and then manufacture victim stories, excuses, cynicism, and coping mechanisms, end up getting sucked into a black hole. Patterns repeat and their negativity becomes a self-fulfilling prophecy of poor results and bad luck.

Sure, Lance got better quickly (he got a clean bill of health only months after his initial diagnosis) and then floated along to fame and fortune after that. However, Lance has faced setbacks, intense criticism, pressure, and controversy along his road to the top of the mountain. In his first professional race, the Clasica San Sebastian, he was famously last among 111 competitors, twenty-seven minutes behind the winner. Distraught and wondering about his career decision, he showed his character three days later when he achieved an amazing second place in the prestigious Championship of Zurich professional event. He was fired from his lucrative position on a French team (for being physically unfit!) while lying in his hospital bed fighting for his life. When his treatment concluded and doctors gave him the go-ahead to return to training, Lance called a press conference and announced, "I'm ready," and then waited for the offers to roll in. No one jumped at the chance, even though he was America's brightest star and one of the best, if not *the* best, one-day racer in the world before his illness.

It was the fledgling U.S. Postal Service–sponsored team that was the only outfit willing to risk a contract on Lance in 1998. His salary went from $1.2 million with the French Cofidis team to a $200,000 base with the U.S. Postal Service team. Fortunately, Bill Stapleton was savvy enough to add a bonus clause for accumulating UCI points (cycling's international performance ranking system, encompassing all major races) at $1,000 per point. Lance had a banner year, with highlights like fourth in the Tour of Spain and fourth in the World Championships, earning an outstanding eight hundred UCI points. The windfall due per his contract, which far exceeded the team's modest budget, was personally guaranteed with great pleasure by a wealthy benefactor of American cycling and part owner of the team named Thom Weisel.

After becoming Tour de France champion, Lance faced endless doping accusations and other attacks on his character, the perceived betrayal by former teammates and business associates, severed love relationships no doubt of magnified stress due to his celebrity, and the daily challenge of living such a high-stakes life.

Honest, Correct, and Real

I pressed to discover how Lance handled some of the speed bumps, such as the rejection from cycling teams upon his comeback. "It was difficult to stay optimistic but fortunately that thing worked out quickly. I settled into a home, into a team, and then it was time to start moving forward quickly," remembers Lance.

"In the case of the negative things written about me, there are certain things in life you can't control. The only thing for me to do is to be honest, correct, and real—to be real with the press. I think that's what the people want to see; I think they appreciate that. Nobody's ever 100 percent popular or 100 percent approved of. The key is to know that it's impossible to be liked by everyone all the time."

Yes, it's impossible to be liked by everyone all the time. That is a difficult thing to internalize and accept. Lots of us run around trying to be liked by everyone, a futile pursuit that often leads to frustration and exhaustion and compromises our ability to retain a positive attitude. The harried modern mom syndrome is a clear example of this issue. Today we have the first generation of mothers who have been in the workforce hard core before bringing a baby into the world. Stay-at-home moms have to downshift from a high-flying career to baby talk, often misapplying their competitive workplace skills to the child-rearing challenge. On the other hand, most working moms have a daily routine that amounts to an exhausting juggling act.

"THE ONLY THING FOR ME TO DO IS TO BE HONEST, CORRECT, AND REAL."

—Lance Armstrong

If your plan of attack in either role is to try and be superwoman—raise perfect kids, have a rewarding career, volunteer for the PTA, and, oh yeah, be fit and sexy, too—the vicious, judgmental modern world will shoot you down with a tranquilizer gun. If your life is physically wearing you out because you are trying to bite off more than you can chew, a positive attitude cannot overcome that. A better choice would be to be honest, realistic, and vulnerable in your approach to life. Academy Award–winning actress and screenwriter Emma Thompson says, "There's no question that parenting is wonderful, but it's also difficult, tiring, and boring." If you can be OK with the fact that you can't achieve perfection and if you can maintain a sense of humor when things don't go exactly as planned, you are on your way to becoming a good parent and a positive person.

Sometimes you are going to have to tell your kids "no" and let them cry and scream that you are a terrible mommy or daddy. It's important to express your love by showing them a world with firm boundaries and expectations. For kids to battle you is a natural part of life; what's unnatural is for everything to go smoothly and for kids to always get their way. Sometimes you are going to have to show your real face at work and explain to your boss that real life may actually compromise your performance at times because you can't be in two places at once. If he or she gives you grief, you must be comfortable being assertive and understanding that compromise is a part of life. Perhaps, instead of feeling conflicted and stressed about being pulled in different directions, you can feel privileged to be wanted in different areas. If your boss tries to manipulate, intimidate, or guilt you into compromising your values, personal life, or general health, you must be comfortable and confident in asserting your priorities. And you must be prepared to take action to reclaim what is rightfully yours: a healthy, happy, positive, and balanced life.

This is a more empowering choice than becoming a victim of a guilt-and-manipulation game to get you to overextend yourself yet again. You may "look good" climbing the corporate ladder by being on the conference call instead of at your kid's piano recital, but you may regret this strategy later. If you are able to be eternally positive and open-minded, you can create a world of infinite possibilities and more favorable options than the black-and-white options we are often deceived with or intimidated into. Maybe you can negotiate a rescheduling of the conference call. After all, your coworkers may have kids playing piano or baseball, too.

In Austin Murphy's 2006 *Sports Illustrated* cover story about Lance's new career, cancer advocacy, Lance's pal Bono (the Irish front man for the megaband U2 and champion political activist) says, "Most people don't believe that the world should be changed. Lance is different. He understands that hills can be climbed, and he isn't depressed when, upon reaching the summit of one, he sees a larger one [ahead]. He's used to that. That's what Lance Armstrong stands for."

No Bad Air

The European cycling press, particularly the French press, has been a difficult element in Lance's life. Because of the serious, long-standing problems with doping in professional cycling, Lance has faced endless scrutiny and innuendo from opportunistic journalists regarding the source of his miraculous performances. Despite being tested more often and with more sophisticated methods than perhaps any other athlete in the world, and always coming up clean, Lance, as cycling's most prominent rider, suffered the fallout from the cloud that hangs over professional cycling. His strategy of being honest, correct, and real did little to alleviate the endless controversy that dogged him.

"HE UNDERSTANDS THAT HILLS CAN BE CLIMBED, AND HE ISN'T DEPRESSED WHEN, UPON REACHING THE SUMMIT OF ONE, HE SEES A LARGER ONE [AHEAD]."

—Bono

Sure, "nobody's ever 100 percent popular," but this drama went far beyond that. Some of the attacks were particularly vicious, such as the accusations delivered by Greg LeMond. LeMond was Lance's predecessor as America's top professional cyclist. He won the Tour de France three times (1986, 1989, and 1990), the first such successes by an American in a European sport dominated by Europeans. LeMond also refined the level of professionalism in cycling by successfully negotiating tremendous increases in salary from the traditional blue-collar wages of professional cyclists in

Europe and becoming a familiar corporate pitchman—Americanizing a very provincial sport and blazing a distinct trail for Lance to follow.

LeMond was a brash, opinionated, and very talented champion who rewrote the rules of cycling by breaking long-standing training and lifestyle traditions and winning his way. He had a dramatic comeback from a near-fatal hunting accident to win his second and third Tour de France. Sound like a familiar story? For years Lance maintained a cordial, respectful relationship with LeMond, referring to him as a role model and duly crediting him for his pioneering role in the cycling world.

"THE BIGGEST THING THAT MADE LANCE A CHAMPION WAS HIS LEVEL OF DESIRE, WHICH WAS EXTRAORDINARILY HIGH AND UNWAVERING."

—Mark Gorski

Then in the afterglow of Lance's 2001 Tour victory came some highly controversial comments by LeMond that received big play in the cycling as well as the mainstream press. Basically, LeMond questioned the validity of Lance's performance due to his association with Dr. Ferrari, who had recently been indicted on accusations of dispensing the performance-enhancing, red blood cell–boosting drug erythropoietin (EPO). LeMond said that he was "disappointed" in Armstrong and would "reserve judgment" on Lance's Tour victory until Ferrari's trial was complete. "If Armstrong's clean, it's the greatest comeback. And if he's not, then it's the greatest fraud," LeMond commented.

THE LANCE FACTOR

L ance's positive attitude and singular focus naturally rubbed off on his teammates and his entire organization. Mark Gorski, former managing director of the U.S. Postal Service cycling team and 1984 Olympic gold medalist in track cycling, remembers, "The biggest thing that made Lance a champion was his level of desire, which was extraordinarily high and unwavering. Day after day, year after year, he wanted it more than anyone. You'd think he'd have slipped at some point, with all the money and the titles he'd ever want. But every single day he delivered. He was more focused, trained harder, and wanted to win more than anyone in the sport.

"When you're on a team with someone like that, it can't help but rub off. Just like in the workplace, if you are on a project with a colleague who is incredibly motivated and focused, you are drawn into that level of intensity and positive energy. Lance's leadership role on the team was totally natural and was broad reaching. Yes, he was the selected athlete for the race victory, the designated team leader on the road, but his leadership role was more comprehensive than that. He was a motivational force, and he brought out the best in everyone in the organization—riders, bike mechanics, staff, coaches, sponsors—everyone," Gorski notes.

"He would get in someone's face if he deserved it, but he also knew how to be supportive of a teammate who was struggling," continues Gorski. "Lance had input on rider selection for races, signing new riders, and competitive strategy in the races. This is unusual for a rider to be involved at this level, and there was nothing formal about this role—it was just Lance being Lance. During our time together, Lance was constantly in motion, always wanting to know what was happening and to help make the team better. One year he was watching the Paris-Robaix race [a prestigious single-day race in France that was not on Lance's race schedule but that the U.S. Postal Service team competed in] on live television and called Johan [Bruyneel, who drives the team car on the racecourse and dictates strategy to the riders via two-way radio] on the cell phone to give his tactical input!

"The effect Lance had on his teammates is amazing," Gorski remarks. "Each of his Tour de France teammates was very, very motivated to perform for him, to bring him to victory in the Tour de France. For example, the level of tension and anxiety on team time trial day at the Tour was always incredible."

For years, one stage of the Tour was always a team time trial, where each nine-rider team sets off on a staggered start and rides in formation to cover the course as quickly as possible. Then all team members are assigned the team finish time against their individual accumulated time for the overall race. Lance and his teammates would typically win or come very close to winning, in the process gaining critical time advantages over some of Lance's main rivals on teams who rode slower. In 2004 the Tour de France organizers preposterously changed the rules to establish maximum time losses teams could suffer relative to the fastest team (regardless of how far behind they actually were), a thinly veiled attempt to minimize one of Lance's perennial advantages. In 2006 they departed from tradition and canceled the event from the program!

Gorski continues, "Lance's teammates were deathly afraid of getting dropped on the time trial and hurting Lance's chances. There was absolutely no question in the minds of every member of the team that they would devote every ounce of energy in their bodies to work for Lance in his quest for the yellow jersey."

Dr. Ferrari is a renowned expert on lactate testing, altitude training, nutrition, recovery, and many other aspects of cycling performance and has long been a central figure in the performance evolution of many top pro cyclists. Guilt by association in this case is as reasonable as calling someone who listens to rap music a gangster. Due to LeMond's stature in the sport and Lance's existing relationship with him, the comments came as a shock to Lance, to say the least.

Soon after the predictable firestorm hit LeMond for his unfair and ill-advised comments, he issued an apology, backpedaling so blatantly that it further tarnished his credibility. "I want to be clear that I believe Lance to be a great champion," LeMond said, "and I do not believe, in any way, that he has ever used any performance-enhancing substances." Those who felt like this resonated off-key were keen to note that Trek Bicycles, the sponsor of Lance and the U.S. Postal Service team, also owned a subsidiary brand of bicycles by the name of LeMond. It would not be a stretch to imagine certain interested parties politely twisting LeMond's arm into the shape of an olive branch.

Lance calmly let the situation take care of itself. Millions saw him mention on "Late Show with David Letterman" that he chose to take the "high road" in this situation. His harshest words on the entire subject were that he was "surprised" about LeMond's comments. He offered flowery praise about LeMond and his legacy: "Greg is a friend of mine, someone I respect immensely. I would not be sitting where I am, talking about my sport, without him. I owe him a lot." In this case the high road offered the expected karmic payoff. Three years later (after three more Tour de France wins by Lance), LeMond again had difficulty keeping his mouth shut. "Lance is ready to do anything to protect his secret, but I don't know how he will manage to keep on convincing everybody he is innocent," LeMond said. Rather than dragging Lance down, LeMond's commentary helped to further taint his once-grand legacy with the smell of sour grapes.

Superhuman Versus Superhuman

What about these serious doping accusations by LeMond and others that have dogged Lance throughout his career? First off, the question is not as simple as wondering "did he or didn't he?" about an individual athlete. Major professional sports, including cycling, are infested with performance-enhancing drugs and have been for years. This is mostly thanks to the collective greed of owners or organizers, fans, and athletes who value record-breaking performances more than clean performances. Asking athletes to be deterred by morality is problematic for a couple of reasons. First, when it's clear one's peers are cheating, the level of performance required to survive or excel professionally practically mandates doping. It's either that or stay clean, likely get beaten by athletes with an unfair advantage, and get sent home to toil on the family farm. Regarding the "drugs are dangerous/unhealthy" potential deterrent, the sad truth is that many athletes have shown little regard for their health, or long-term health consequences, when it comes to pursuing peak performance.

A successful professional athlete has to be a risk-taking, narrowminded, fearless being. These traits do not quite jibe with having the restraint and high moral character to "just say no." Furthermore, a cyclist hopped up on steroids and EPO arguably can minimize the brutal physical damage of racing a three-week Tour de France because he can train harder, recover faster, and deliver oxygen to working muscles more efficiently. No, it's not healthy to take drugs, but neither is it healthy to race the Tour de France.

That's the distressing news. The good news is that there are many athletes who have eschewed the doping route and cleanly compete at a high level. And there are compelling reasons to believe in the purity of these elite performers. Like the punch line of Lance's popular Nike commercial went, "Everyone wants to know what I'm on. I'm on my bike six hours a day. What are *you* on?" Marketing glitz to be sure, but in light of the suspicions Lance had to endure, it's a deeply revealing statement that demands sincere reflection. We have zero proof of

> ## "EVERYONE WANTS TO KNOW WHAT I'M ON. I'M ON MY BIKE SIX HOURS A DAY. WHAT ARE *YOU* ON?"
>
> —Lance Armstrong

Lance doping, but we do have conclusive proof that he trained harder than any other professional cyclist in the history of the sport and has extraordinary genetic gifts. Here is an excerpt from a seven-year study on Lance conducted by the University of Texas (Austin) Human Performance Laboratory's Dr. Edward Coyle ("Improved Muscular Efficiency Displayed as Tour de France Champion Matures," printed in the *Journal of Applied Physiology*, June 2005):

> During the months leading up to each of his Tour de France victories, he reduced body weight and body fat by 4–7 kg (i.e., approximately 7 percent). Therefore, over the seven-year period, an improvement in muscular efficiency and reduced body fat contributed equally to a remarkable 18 percent improvement in his steady state power per kg body weight when cycling at a given VO_2. It appears that [even] in the detrained state, this individual's VO_2 max is in the range of the highest values that normal men can achieve with training.

Bart Knaggs laments that the broad audience misses the most profound and complex insights about Lance's magical performances. "Everybody wants to just take this stuff at face value. Maybe they don't have the depth of understanding of the work that an athlete does or understand how complicated the Tour de France is. We think we understand what human performance potential is, and then Lance delivers a performance that is beyond their experience," explains Knaggs.

Could LeMond's accusations have resulted from a disbelief that Lance could climb the fabled eleven kilometers [about seven miles] up to Alpe d'Huez in thirty-eight minutes, while LeMond's best time in the Tour was forty-eight minutes? Irish journalist David Walsh and French journalist Pierre Ballester wrote an entire book (*L.A. Confidentiel*, printed in French) advancing their own opinions that point to Lance's guilt. These included his guilt-by-association relationship with Dr. Ferrari and other gems, like Walsh's comment on the fact that the 1999 Tour de France field completed the course at a faster average speed than in 1998, a year in which the event was tainted by a huge rider drug bust. "How can clean racers ride faster than those known to be on dope?" Huh? Perhaps the same way honest businesspeople can make more money than crooked ones?

In *Outside* magazine's comprehensive December 2005 article "J'Accuse," this conclusion about *L.A. Confidentiel* was offered: "The end result is a sprawling collection of interviews, statistics, timelines, and newspaper accounts, but no proof against Armstrong. . . . On the whole, because Walsh and Ballester's evidence in the book is circumstantial, no single piece of it has the power of truth." My account of Lance hammering his mountain bike up a mountain in October could be far more relevant than Walsh's rubbish about average racing speeds of the Tour pack or the highly questionable testimony from former employees and teammates to circumstantial evidence of doping by Lance.

Even into retirement, Lance remained hounded by allegations that surfaced during a 2005 trial over an insurance company's refusal to pay a $5 million Tour de France victory bonus to him. The story was farcical but distressingly still made headlines. Confidential testimony was leaked to the media, including more allegations from LeMond and odd characters such as a former teammate's vindictive wife who offered spotty testimony of Lance admitting to a room full of listeners to illegal doping while in his hospital bed three days after brain surgery (she was also discovered to have conferred with and assisted the insurance company). The insurance company eventually coughed up the $5 million, plus a $2.5 million penalty.

Suspicion may continue in the minds of some, particularly with the sport continuing to be disgraced by widespread doping. In 2006 nine riders were expelled just before the start of the Tour due to a doping scandal involving a Spanish physician. Included in the list were the top two favorites for 2006 and two of Lance's main rivals during his reign: German Jan Ullrich and Italian Ivan Basso. Floyd Landis's dramatic victory was tainted by a positive drug test.

There are two factors that strongly support Lance as a clean performer. First, Lance is a genetically superior athlete who competed at an elite professional level for nearly twenty years, beginning with his teenage triathlon career. In 1993 (before drugs like EPO rose to prominence in cycling) at the age of twenty-one, he blasted away from cycling's greatest stars on the rainy roads of Oslo, Norway—including five-time Tour de France winner Miguel Indurain—to win the world championship. Dopers are literally trying to obtain Lance's natural body chemistry, which was revealed at the age of sixteen, when he raced the world's top triathletes; at twenty-one, when he ascended to the highest level of cycling; and into his thirties, as he won the Tour year after year.

Perhaps the most compelling factor that proves Lance's innocence is a *disincentive* to cheat that dwarfs that of anyone else in cycling or any other sport. Lance transcended cycling to become a cultural icon and earned perhaps ten times that of the next-best-paid cycling superstar. Stapleton reminds us that Lance's team contracts and endorsement contracts have always had clauses in them that state a positive drug test is grounds for termination. Lance's hypothetical dilemma is a little different from that of a desperate journeyman struggling to hold down his position in the pro pack or even a star entrenched in the European cycling culture. The threat of a two-year doping suspension is a stiff penalty, to be sure, but moderate in terms of the risk versus reward.

Retired French great Richard Virenque, the record holder for the most (seven) "King of the Mountain" titles in the Tour de France (similar to the yellow jersey reward for the overall fastest time, this polka-dot jersey is earned by scoring points for high placement on mountain climbs over the course of the Tour), was implicated in the 1998 doping scandal that nearly shut down the Tour. Virenque issued repeated denials in the face of mounting evidence and confessions of those around him. His "*à l'insu de mon plein gré*" ("without the knowledge of my own will") defense was so preposterous that, as Wikipedia.com explains, "this phrase soon passed into French popular culture as a sign of hypocritical denial."

Virenque finally confessed, served out a doping suspension, and returned to earn more titles at the Tour. In the 2002 Tour Virenque climbed away from Lance to victory on the legendary Mount Ventoux stage amid a tremendous reception from the fans. Meanwhile, two minutes in arrear, Lance endured repeated catcalls of "*Dopé!*" ("Doper!") during his ascent. This contrast in reception offers a keen psychological insight into the French mentality that has driven the enduring persecution of Lance during and after his Tour de France reign. "I am sorry, but with Virenque we have the biggest rogue in the last fifty years of doping," Lance told the Belgian newspaper *Het Nieuwsblad* in 2005.

If Lance had been caught for doping, however, a two-year suspension would have been the least of his worries. He would have been disgraced by perhaps the biggest doping story in sports history and literally pissed away tens of millions of dollars from American Century Investments, Subaru, Nike, Bristol-Myers Squibb, Trek, 24 Hour Fitness, Coca-Cola, Oakley, and other corporate partners. He would have decimated large enterprises like Discovery Channel Pro Cycling and Capital Sports and Entertainment (which together employ nearly one hundred people), along with the Lance Armstrong Foundation cancer charity. He would have kids (and grown-ups) in cancer wards crying and confused about their hero being a cheater.

He would have been economically, socially, and morally destroyed ("the three basic flavors of incentives," says the book *Freakonomics*— or disincentives, in this case) as an athlete and as a person.

We must collectively look beyond the basic symptoms of a problem as complex as doping and reflect deeper, measuring our thoughts and words carefully. Fans, administrators, and athletes must all draw a hard line against doping in sports but at the same time take care not to cross the line and taint clean performances with flawed accusations. The great British middle-distance runner and Olympic gold medalist Sebastian Coe said, "You've got to be careful pointing fingers at people making big breakthroughs, because only in public terms is it a big breakthrough. In reality, the athlete has been slogging away, mile after mile, weight after weight, for ten years at a time."

The Air Filter

"With the LeMond situation, it really backfired for him. I knew that would happen," Lance reflects. "Outside commentary, outside events—these things I can't control. I do lose sleep over them at times, because I care. But you have to prioritize these things—think less about the bad stuff. Your personal time, your personal space, your rest and recovery are important. Worrying about things you can't control can hamper these.

"I don't like negative air. I don't like bad air!" Lance expands on his point emphatically. "I don't like being around negative situations or negative people. And I don't have to anymore. That's the great thing; if I don't want to be someplace, I just get up and walk out!"

While few would admit that they enjoy bad air, it's easy to get into the habit of breathing it daily and spreading it around to others. You don't like it but you can't help living mired in it on a day-to-day basis. We all know how it feels to be criticized—by loved ones or in a public situation like an important meeting in the conference room. Even when the stakes are relatively low, it's easy to allow unpleasant situations or comments to ruin your day, erode your self-confidence, and keep you trapped in a cycle of negative communication and behavior patterns.

"I DON'T LIKE NEGATIVE AIR. I DON'T LIKE BAD AIR!"

—Lance Armstrong

Anyone who has had a failed or struggling relationship knows how difficult it is to redirect negative energy. Now imagine being a celebrity where your work is criticized, or harmful gossip is spread, in worldwide media instead of some anonymous office break room. It's harder to walk away from bad air when the whole world is breathing it! The essence of Lance's recovery message is to gain strength from negative experiences so that you may live stronger in the present. This is an appealing alternative to feeling sorry for yourself.

Lance's secret to dealing with the stress of being on top is that he filters out the bad air and breathes only the clean air. He developed a positive attitude so resilient and a perspective so enlightened that he could rise above the chatter around him, pedal his bike through all kinds of adversity and obstacles, and emerge victorious. I asked him if his cancer experience helps him put the ups and downs of life in perspective. "Everything in life gets compared to the all-time lows and the all-time highs, whether it's an athlete's performance or a stock price. I can compare my own life experience to the all-time lows of '96. It is a very healthy, rewarding feeling to know that I've been to hell and back. I was absolutely a stronger rider mentally for having been to a really bad place, a really low place. Struggling in training and competition, bad weather, bad life circumstances—I'm not saying they have no effect. I absolutely get pissed about certain things, just less so than before. But I have created a bigger filter, a better filter, so I can recover faster from setbacks," Lance explains.

LANCE'S SECRET TO DEALING WITH THE STRESS OF BEING ON TOP IS THAT HE FILTERS OUT THE BAD AIR AND BREATHES ONLY THE CLEAN AIR.

Those who saw or read about Lance's victory in the spectacular time trial stage up the famed Alpe d'Huez mountain in the 2004 Tour should note that the mountain was only one of Lance's challenges that day. As he ascended the open roads of the nine-mile mountain climb amid nine hundred thousand rabid fans, he had residing in the back of his mind a death threat that had been issued on the eve of the race. With police sharpshooters riding in his team follow car (bumping the usual occupants, like corporate sponsor big shots and rock star girlfriends), Lance had to filter out this distraction and ascend through a mob of fervently nationalistic fans, many unruly and drunken, who clogged the roadway screaming, spitting, and parting only at the very last moment to allow for a bicycle-width opening up the road. Athletes in mainstream sports, performing in the confines of secure stadiums and arenas, could not dream of a situation with as much pressure.

Filter in this context can mean many things. There is a physical, tangible filter of eliminating distractions to use your time wisely and effectively. This would include turning off your addictive instant e-mail messaging screen to complete a written presentation, getting out of bed for a morning run, or passing on dessert to stay committed to your diet goals. There is also an emotional filter, where you allow criticism, negative energy, and difficult experiences to roll off you and not affect your present or future disposition.

Lance's choice of the word *filter* is apropos of the chaotic and multifaceted life he lived during his cycling career and that he continues to live. The tightrope act that was Lance's career seemed to him to be strung one foot off the ground. If you were to sub in someone else—anyone else—for Lance, the tightrope would appear to be strung across Niagara Falls. During Lance's reign as Tour de France champ, he also wore hats of cancer spokesperson, corporate pitchman, de facto chief executive of a multimillion-dollar business entity, member of the jet set with rock-star former partner Sheryl Crow, and, finally, regular guy trying to raise a family. Lance's grand life distinguished him from nearly all of his peers in the ranks of professional athletes. There were some cycling rivals who could hang with Lance pretty well, but no one can truly hang with Lance's lifestyle.

Most pro athletes lead such insular, one-dimensional lives that there is basically nothing to filter out. Many believe that doing anything beyond reclining horizontally compromises performance and recovery. In a 2004 *Sacramento Bee* article chronicling a "day in the life" of Sacramento Kings NBA rookie Kevin Martin, he culminated a day of reckless driving, mindless errands, and conspicuous consumption by retiring to his crib to play a basketball video game where he could choose himself as the protagonist. A humorous passage in Daniel Coyle's *Lance Armstrong's War* relates some popular cyclist superstitions such as pushing elevator buttons with the elbow to avoid germs and going to ridiculous lengths to avoid walking or standing to alleviate stress on the muscles.

As we learned from the Palm Springs convention day, Lance thrives on being constantly in motion, tackling different challenges, and leading a multidimensional life. I believe that this kind of balance is healthy for an athlete and that the chillin' horizontal crowd can learn something from Lance's example. Lying around all day obsessing about an upcoming race or workout can create stress and anxiety in an idle mind. Furthermore, the more insular and one-dimensional people are, the easier it is for them to get thrown off center and stress out when life does not unfold exactly as they want. If you are a cyclist freaked out about standing for too long, doing so will produce stress and anxiety. If you are so self-absorbed that your sole contribution to the planet is scoring baskets for your team and your leisure time is spent scoring electronic baskets for your video-game team, you are falling short of being a champion in the broad sense embodied by Lance.

Lance was able to thrive in a chaotic life because he enjoyed it and maintained a positive attitude in the face of stimuli that would overwhelm any mortal. The universal challenge of wearing many hats was handled deftly by Lance, despite having to wear more hats than just about anyone else. While Stapleton describes him as always being informed about every business or team matter on the table, in the next breath we learn how Lance would annually shut off his connection to the outside world when he engaged in the crucial final weeks of preparation for the Tour. Lance's furious off-season schedule of private jet travel from one gig to the next, constant cell phone and BlackBerry use, and aggressive compression of sensible time-lines to squeeze in daily bike rides bore little resemblance to his June daily routine, where his only hat was a bike helmet and his longest training sessions stretched to eight hours—the winning formula to get his body to peak condition on the Tour starting line.

The Age of Interruption

Lance's master multitasking ability is actually better described as an ability to completely focus and absorb himself in a single activity. The truth is that multitasking is a myth and misnomer. As Stapleton explains, Lance's ability to compartmentalize and switch quickly

LANCE TIME

How does Lance balance his complex, multifaceted life? Bill Stapleton offers this explanation: "Lance is one in a billion—one of the most complicated, multitasking individuals I've ever seen. His ability to compartmentalize is incredible. He can go effortlessly from LAF [Lance Armstrong Foundation] issues, to family time, to training time, to 'Stapleton, what's up with this deal?' time. Lance also operates in another dimension of time. I'll look at an impossibly scheduled daily agenda—'do this at 1 P.M., be here at 1:45 P.M., and so on'—and I'll think, 'What about travel time? How are we going to get all this done?' But time just warps for him; he pulls it off every time. Lance gets twelve things done in a day where I think we can only do six. I don't know how, but time just slows down for him."

Stapleton continues, "When he lived in Girona [Spain, his European training base in the final years of his career], he'd be out training on the bike for eight hours, then come home and go out to dinner with the family, then get on the computer or phone at night and do business for an hour. Whereas you or I would look at the clock and say, 'Enough, it's bedtime.' For sure, his energy level is super high and his attitude is always positive, which help tremendously."

from divergent tasks is the true recipe for peak performance in varied endeavors. In contrast, many of us succumb to the overwhelming stimulation of the modern world, where multitasking really means parceling out fractions of our full attention in a scattered manner and being unable to focus intently on any one thing for a sustained period. The human brain is not able to truly focus on more than one thing at a time. Yes, you can talk on the phone and make dinner, but handling more than one task requires that the others become mindless. (I guess the mindless task in this example depends on who is calling and what you are making!)

It requires tremendous discipline to focus intently on each successive task or challenge over the course of your day, but it's much better than becoming a victim of today's "Age of Interruption," as *New York Times* columnist Thomas L. Friedman calls it. "Who can think or write or innovate under such conditions [constant interruptions]? One wonders whether the Age of Interruption will lead to a decline in civilization—as ideas and attention spans shrink and we all get diagnosed with some version of Attention Deficit Disorder," Friedman comments. Furthermore, a multitasking, interruptible environment and behavior breeds negativity, is extremely fatiguing, and inhibits peak performance in any one activity.

As we learned earlier at the photo shoot, when Lance is done with something, he is finished and on to the next thing. You can create this reality for yourself with some simple habits: turn off the Black-Berry at your kid's soccer game, exercise first thing in the morning before firing up your computer, respond to old voice mail messages before being distracted by checking new ones, turn off the television during dinner, and so on. By establishing these guidelines and protecting yourself from the pull of a hyperspeed world, you empower yourself and others around you (yes, even little kids: "One moment please, grown-ups are talking") to respect the importance of focusing and remaining in the present.

Fight or Flight

The way we handle the stress of the outside world is based upon our perceptions. Hans Seyle, the father of modern stress research, showed us that stress has three components: stimulus, perception, and response. When we are hiking in the woods and encounter a bear (*stimulus*), we *perceive* a life-threatening situation, and the fight-or-flight *response* is activated in our bodies, so we can run for our lives. This important survival mechanism has been hardwired into our genes since the caveman days as a key survival tool.

Stress in this context really means "stimulation" and can be positive or negative. Today we don't face off with bears very often, but, thanks to technology and industrialization, we do have the unrelenting stimulation of modern life. Someone bustling along in a hectic workplace, an athlete in heavy training, or a college student studying for finals are all asking their bodies to function at a heightened state for an extended period without adequate relief. Eventually, the stress response (the endocrine system flooding the bloodstream with hormones that give us that "adrenaline boost") gives out and you experience exhaustion and burnout. Attitude is a big factor here, too. Provocations such as bad weather, a traffic jam, a flat tire on a training ride, disagreements with people having different points of view, or a lost business deal will trigger the stress response in the body and cause a person to needlessly burn energy fretting about an imperfect world.

When Lance applies the aforementioned physical and emotional filters to his life challenges, he is less impacted on a biochemical level by the damaging effects of stress than a person with a negative or pessimistic disposition. Lance's enjoyment of wearing many hats made his hectic schedule uplifting and energizing instead of exhausting. For an obscure athlete with nothing else to do, it is still difficult to filter out everything—to go to sleep instead of watch a video, shrug off negative feedback and maintain a positive attitude, remain devoted to a long-term training program and not succumb to the pull of ego demands. Such things are what make the difference between a champion and someone who can never quite break through.

Unlike many other athletes, who wilt or freak out under pressure, Lance perceived competitive stimulus in a positive manner, welcoming the intensity of competition and responding accordingly.

It's awe-inspiring for spectators and frustrating for competitors, like French cycling great Laurent Jalabert, who said, "Lance Armstrong seems as if he doesn't feel pain, he's like a machine, like the star of an American film, a Terminator who never dies."

WHEN LANCE APPLIES THE AFOREMENTIONED PHYSICAL AND EMOTIONAL FILTERS TO HIS LIFE CHALLENGES, HE IS LESS IMPACTED ON A BIOCHEMICAL LEVEL BY THE DAMAGING EFFECTS OF STRESS THAN A PERSON WITH A NEGATIVE OR PESSIMISTIC DISPOSITION.

Lance's ability to filter effectively was the result of a maturation process from his early years, where he was heavy on aggression and power and light on patience and reasoning. Thanks to the expert guidance of people like Johan Bruyneel and Chris Carmichael, Lance harnessed his competitive instincts to apply them strategically in competition. When Lance experienced struggles during the Tour, he never panicked or departed from his game plan.

Developing Your Immune System

Consider your own lifestyle, your own workday. When you walk into your office, how is your filter? Are you spending every minute of every day doing the absolute highest-priority tasks to actualize the highest form of your talent? Are you disciplined enough to take regular breaks, eat nutritious food, and preserve your health, energy, and productivity in the face of difficult work circumstances? Or does the constant stimulation and distraction of people and technology inherent in the modern workplace turn you into a victim more concerned with staying afloat than peak performance?

Now let's consider the emotional filter. Eastern philosophy tells us it is best to not be overly concerned with self, to eliminate all influence of the ego, to live for the moment and not fret about the past or future. With a stance like this, you certainly won't wither in the face of criticism, office politics, or codependent relationships. While few people in the modern world are good examples of this, we all have enjoyed glimpses of what it's like to live a more evolved, blissful life. The power of love with a romantic partner or a child helps one maintain an excellent filter in the face of everyday stresses. So does competing at a high level in athletics, backpacking for a week in the mountains, doing volunteer work for the needy, or spending quiet time at the beginning or end of each day to focus on breathing and listening to the sounds of nature. Perspective is available everywhere we look, at all times.

Petty arguments, traffic jams, and declining stock prices don't take that much out of you when you have good mojo going in your life. The problem lies in how easy it is to get thrown off your center. If you are enjoying this book and someone calls to tell you that your credit card is maxed out, you can instantly plunge into a bad mood. Your filter gets tweaked, and negative energy pours in like a flash flood. All of a sudden your perspective is under water. On those occasions where you can't easily walk away (bad air with a boss or loved one, for example), you can rise above the petty emotional games that we all play in our lives—power struggles, guilt manipulations, defensiveness, and rationalizations—and take the high road like Lance did on "Letterman."

As new-age author Don Miguel Ruiz reminds us in *The Four Agreements*, "Don't take anything personally. Nothing others do is because of you. What others say is a projection of their own reality. When you are immune to the opinions and actions of others, you won't be the victim of needless suffering."

If you can grasp the concept that you are always in control of certain elements in your life, like your attitude, you can help get your filter screwed back on tight in an instant. A positive attitude is something that is free for the taking anytime by anyone. Your attitude can be the greatest weapon you have against the challenges of life or your worst enemy, and it is your choice as to which.

To Hell and Back

Not many of us have escaped a brush with death and lived to tell about it. I asked Lance how his survivorship insights can apply to someone without such a dramatic past. "Actually, I think plenty of people have, in one way or another, been to hell and back. Afterward, everything is recalibrated. You look at things differently; your lenses change. My experience with cancer affects every area of my life—family, athletics, business, charity. It's a good thing. I am a better person and have a better perspective."

Linda Armstrong Kelly was similarly affected by her only child enduring his struggle with cancer. "When Lance got sick, that was the turning point in my life," she told me. "All those years, I ran interference for him, managed things for him, and tried to make his life as comfortable as possible. But when he got sick, I realized that this was something I couldn't fix; I couldn't take the disease from him. Since then, I've strived to accept today, be grateful for yesterday, and hope for tomorrow."

Because Lance is totally healthy today, the strength he gains from his cancer experience comes from a memory. Some people do the opposite with a memory—allowing the *memory* of a traumatic experience to torment them indefinitely. While it's certainly hard to let things go sometimes, Lance knows that all he has to do is "switch lenses."

The modern world conditions us to be habitually jealous, envious, and never quite satisfied. The zillion-dollar advertising industry relies heavily on this premise, promising happiness through the purchase of newfangled products or services. Of course, this is the Great American Lie. Some may be confused or even offended to read new-age author and lecturer Dan Millman's admonition to "be happy now, without reason, or you never will be." Upon reflection, a stance like this may be of great value as we become ever more deeply immersed in the melodrama of our daily lives. When the landlord says the rent is late and he might have to litigate, "don't worry, be happy" is tough advice to swallow. The suggestion here is not to roll over, pop open another can of beer, and forget about it. That is the modus operandi of the depressed.

When you can adopt a positive attitude in your daily struggles, you become empowered such that you can emerge victorious over anything. A speaker at the wake of my friend Brice Clark, who passed away in 2005 after a long and painful struggle with cancer, shared an interesting perspective about Brice's battle. "Some will say that Brice lost the battle with cancer, but I don't look at it that way. Cancer didn't beat him. He believed to the very last day that he was going to get better, that the latest new drug or holistic treatment would cure him." By remaining positive in the face of his ordeal, Brice lived the absolute best life he could. In the end, cancer took his life, but it did not crush his spirit.

WHILE IT'S CERTAINLY HARD TO LET THINGS GO SOMETIMES, LANCE KNOWS THAT ALL HE HAS TO DO IS "SWITCH LENSES."

Choosing a positive attitude is no guarantee that you are going to come out on top, but it is a guarantee to help you perform to your potential, face failure and disappointment like a champion, and live a rich, rewarding life. This is true for whatever circumstances you face. Linda Armstrong Kelly claims that "growing up in poverty and having to do without the basic necessities that a lot of people take for granted has made me a stronger person." Others are weakened and demoralized by their bad cards, causing life to deal them more.

It's important to understand that you can receive inspiration and perspective at any time—from your present situation, from a past memory, from someone else's story, or, finally, from the realization that everything can change in an instant. "I think of my husband, Ed Kelly," Linda continues. "He was married for thirty years to a wonderful woman, raised three beautiful, successful children, was a successful businessman—had everything in the world going for him. Then one day his wife gets diagnosed and soon succumbs to cancer. Just like that, in the snap of the fingers, life can quickly change."

STEPS TO DEVELOP SUCCESS FACTOR 1: POSITIVE ATTITUDE

1. Make attitude a choice. Regardless of external circumstances, attitude remains the most powerful and empowering choice you can make. Make the choice to be honest, correct, and real in dealings with yourself and others, especially in the face of difficult circumstances. Cultivate a healthy, balanced lifestyle to support your positive attitude.

2. Avoid "bad air." You can achieve this by calling it out and breaking the cycle of emotional power struggles between loved ones and close associates. Even an innocent comment about the weather contributes to negativity and must be challenged and reframed. Take the high road and remain positive in the face of conflict and challenge. A traffic jam provides an opportunity to relax and reflect on your busy life, a defeat in competition provides an opportunity to learn more about yourself and become a better corporate or athletic performer in the future, and so on.

3. Develop your air filter. In a physical, practical sense, you must prioritize your time and energy and eliminate the distractions that hamper your pursuit of goals and happiness. In an emotional sense, you must move on from difficult experiences, criticism, and other setbacks. Focus on the positive elements of the challenges that you experience and eliminate the negatives. This is especially relevant because we are not perfect. If you enjoy a decadent slice of cheesecake for dessert in conflict with your diet, instead of feeling negative about it, just enjoy it as an element of a happy, balanced life. Then strengthen your commitment to emphasize a diet of healthy, natural foods.

4. Practice. Developing the ability to remain positive requires repetition and reinforcement. Realize that an excessively stressful daily life brings great risk of burnout, exhaustion, and consequent negativity. When you encounter bad air, don't take things personally. Instead, draw strength from negative experiences by letting them go and choosing a positive attitude in the present.

Graham Watson, grahamwatson.com

5

SUCCESS FACTOR 2
CLARITY OF PURPOSE

When Lance left the triathlon circuit at the age of eighteen to pursue a cycling career, I told him he was making a horrible mistake. He was trading a chance to become the top triathlete in the world with a couple more years of development (an assessment I still believe was accurate) for life as an anonymous *domestique* (the French term for a rider in a supporting role to the star of the team, which is how every pro starts his career). By age twenty-one, Lance had risen from a roster guy on a minor-league American team to become the 1993 World Cycling champion, where he upset the five-time Tour de France champion Miguel Indurain of Spain in the annual single-day championship held in Oslo, Norway. He probably could have purchased the sport of triathlon whole with his ensuing windfall.

After Lance achieved that 1993 victory, I remarked to fellow pro triathlete Rip Esselstyn, an Austin resident and occasional winter training partner of Lance's, that Lance must be beside himself with such an incredible result. Esselstyn countered, "No, no, no, no! You don't understand Lance. He's not satisfied with the world title. He always wants more, more, more. Next he will probably want to win the Tour!"

Back in 1993 this was a preposterous comment. Lance had been pegged as the most aggressive and explosive rider the pro cycling ranks had perhaps ever seen, with the perfect temperament and physical makeup to win single-day races. This single-day "classic" rider profile is quite different from the riders who excel in three-week Tours, who tend to be slighter in frame (the better to carry up the high mountains) and more patient and strategic in mind-set. As the world knows, Lance made that dramatic and improbable evolution in his physique, temperament, and performance goals to become the greatest Tour rider in history.

Hiking and Cell Phones

Clarity of purpose comes when you are pursuing the highest expression of your talents, are motivated primarily by the love of your activity, and live a lifestyle congruent with your stated purpose. When you have clarity of purpose, you will do whatever it takes to achieve your goals—and you will love every minute of it. For example, let's say you decide to spend a summer hiking the 211-mile John Muir Trail in the Sierra Nevada of California, "an area," according to GORP.com (an outdoor recreation resource website), "that many backpackers agree is the finest mountain scenery in the United States. A land blessed with the mildest, sunniest climate of any major mountain range in the world." Sounds like fun, so you log on to the GORP site and discover that "the Muir Trail is not a place to hike on impulse. Its length, remoteness, and great changes in altitude mean that you must plan your hike if you are going to enjoy it, or even to complete it."

With your purpose clearly defined, you go about preparations for the big adventure. As you read on, you discover that you'll need to ship food and supplies to yourself, picking up your care packages at a few key locations where civilization can be found in a detour a few miles off the trail. You'll need to be prepared for "how your emotions might react to various backpacking situations [like] solitude (if you go alone), enforced togetherness (if you don't go alone), cold, hunger and injury." Finally, with your backpack stocked full of maps and supplies and perhaps joined by carefully chosen companions, you head out. Each day, you start at one red dot on the map and reach another that is ever closer to your final destination—as straightforward an endeavor as you can get. Perhaps it's because of their straightforward nature that we enjoy simple physical pursuits like hiking, running, or cycling.

Daily life is not like a trail hike. Instead of a focused, linear procession to our goals, we are bombarded with excessive stimulus that can and does distract us endlessly. The harmful influences of materialism and consumerism pull us away from feeling clarity and doing things for the love of the experience, luring us instead into megamalls where we can supposedly purchase happiness and self-esteem for ourselves and our loved ones.

Technological advancements continue to disrespect the natural balance of stress and rest that our bodies crave, in favor of keeping us "connected" and entertained at all times. Recently a friend (let's protect his identity by calling him Duane) received a cell phone call from his mom while driving along in Southern California traffic. She was calling to alert him of a *Los Angeles Times* newspaper article detailing the danger of talking on the cell phone while driving. "Hmm, hold on a sec," said Duane. His mom waited, hearing what sounded like crinkling paper in the background. Duane came back: "Oh yes, here's the article."

TECHNOLOGICAL ADVANCEMENTS CONTINUE TO DISRESPECT THE NATURAL BALANCE OF STRESS AND REST THAT OUR BODIES CRAVE.

The flawed mentality of the rat race values a superficial kind of success, causing many to suppress their hopes, dreams, and reflections on how they are spending their life. Are you doing your absolute best in every role that you play? Is your career reflecting your special talents and passion such that you are making the most significant contribution possible to the world? Or do you feel stuck in a rut of responsibilities or victim stories with a sense that something is missing or you are lacking direction? Are you taking the absolute best care of your health, understanding that it is the most valuable asset that you will ever have? Or are you watching idly as the aging process runs its course?

We all dream about doing great things with our lives, exploring our special talents, or answering the call to do something meaningful and exciting. Regardless of what your current situation is, gaining clarity of purpose can help you unleash your potential and powerfully influence the lives of others. As Martin Luther King Jr. said,

> If a man is to be called a street sweeper, he should sweep streets as Michelangelo painted, or Beethoven composed music or Shakespeare wrote poetry. He should sweep streets so well that all the hosts of heaven and earth will pause to say, "Here lived a great street sweeper who did his job well."

For Love or Money?

Lance Armstrong believed deeply that the highest expression of his talent as a human being and greatest impact he could have on society was to be a champion in his sport of destiny. This was his all-consuming life purpose, pursued with intensity unimaginable to the average person or even most of his competition. Over the course of his career, he created a lifestyle ideally suited to achieving his goals, understanding the importance of balance, sacrifice, patience, and decision making uncluttered by distraction or superficial motivations.

Without this clarity of purpose, he would not have made it or stayed at the top for any length of time—the sacrifice was too intense to pursue and maintain dominance. Despite the incredible amount of suffering and difficult physical work involved, Lance stated repeatedly that he loved all aspects of his cycling career. Just as the street sweeper can take inspiration from Michelangelo, athletes and nonathletes alike can all relate to the passion Lance showed for riding his bicycle and implement the success factor of clarity of purpose to enrich their own lives.

"Early in my career, my purpose for competing was—like most young people—money," Lance reveals. "When I enjoyed some good luck with financial success, I can honestly say that money was no longer the main motivation. I don't think it should be for an athlete, or anyone else for that matter. The motivation I had early in my career was effective, but it wasn't very healthy or long lasting. If I had remained motivated primarily by money, I would have burned out long before winning the Tour de France seven times. My motivation evolved to something deeper and longer lasting—my love for the sport: the training, the competition, and the pursuit of excellence as a professional cyclist."

Because love of the sport was Lance's primary motivator, he was able to maintain a healthy perspective about his athletic career. He didn't equate results with self-esteem. He possessed a higher purpose than just winning—motivating and inspiring millions and serving as a role model for sportsmanship, dedication, and commitment, particularly to the cancer community. Feeling this clear and higher purpose became a source of power when he faced challenging circumstances. Rather than choke or withdraw under pressure, he felt the freedom to give his best effort.

Furthermore, having a clear purpose for pursuing goals is the key to maintaining extremely high motivation levels, even after tremendous success makes superficial motivators like wealth and glory an afterthought. "When Lance came back after cancer, he had a higher purpose in his life for the first time," Bart Knaggs remembers. "People crave purpose, a sense of belonging to a community or bigger cause. Before cancer, Lance never had this. He had minimal family ties and lived a transient lifestyle—traveling all over for races, spending part of the year in Texas and part in Italy, then moving to France, and so on. Then, all of the sudden, he gets a sense of nobility and embarks on a hero's journey. He wanted to show the world that he could recover from being a white, pasty, bald cancer victim to become the best cyclist in the world."

"IF I HAD REMAINED MOTIVATED PRIMARILY BY MONEY, I WOULD HAVE BURNED OUT LONG BEFORE WINNING THE TOUR DE FRANCE SEVEN TIMES. MY MOTIVATION EVOLVED TO SOMETHING DEEPER AND LONGER LASTING— MY LOVE FOR THE SPORT."

—Lance Armstrong

"When I needed to be motivated, I never lacked it," Lance explained about his cycling career. "During the off-season, I was certainly not motivated to go out and do six weeks of heavy, intense training, but I didn't need to either. Having the balance of an off-season and regularly programmed downtime enabled me to never have to struggle for motivation when I needed it. You have to know when to step on the gas and when to brake. Now if I couldn't find motivation in May [a crucial training period for the July Tour de France], that would have been a real problem. But it never happened.

When you work hard for something and achieve it, you get the prize of time off, of being able to create your own schedule, to rewrite the rules [of cycling]," Lance explains.

Pro cyclists typically are required by their teams to race 150-plus days per year over an eight- to nine-month season. Lance raced maybe fifty days a year over a competitive season happening over roughly a four-month period (April through July). During that competitive season, his sole focus was the Tour de France. He allowed all of the other races to serve as tune-up events, with his finishing results of minor concern. Nevertheless, in 2001 he earned the world's number one ranking in a point system that encompasses all races.

For Instance, a Balanced Life

It's certainly easier to be high-minded and put love ahead of money when you are making eighteen million bucks a year, but Lance explains that it was his cancer ordeal more than a swelling bank account that altered his perspective. "After my illness, money and the acquiring of material goods just didn't seem as important. It helped me realize there is more to life than earning money and the things that come with that—your neighborhood, the car you drive, that kind of thing. I work hard and, of course, like to get paid for what I do, but money isn't the primary motivator."

"AFTER MY ILLNESS, MONEY AND
THE ACQUIRING OF MATERIAL GOODS
JUST DIDN'T SEEM AS IMPORTANT."

—Lance Armstrong

In contrast, many of us struggle with motivation levels, perhaps because the clarity of purpose and pure love for our activities is clouded by superficial goals and ego demands. Many in the rat race sell out their families. Witness corporate legend and longtime GE boss Jack Welch lamenting in his autobiography *Jack: Straight from the Gut* that he regrets not leading a balanced life.

"Not coincidentally, my direct reports showed up [to work on Saturdays] too," says Welch. "It's clear that the balance I chose had consequences for the people around me at home and at the office. For instance, my kids were raised, largely alone, by their mother. . . . If there was ever a case of 'Do as I say, not as I did,' this is it." *Hint:* if you are living a lifestyle that seems out of balance and that you think you might regret someday or if you refer to your relationship with your kids as a "for instance," you may be struggling with clarity of purpose.

Reception on the Green

Many fail to recognize that no one can or should even try to be "on" all the time, like the guy who answers his cell phone on the golf course. Being a traditionalist who grew up in a family of competitive golfers, I have a perspective about the sport that may be a little different from the cigar-smoking, beer-guzzling, hot dog–scarfing crowd who seem to have christened golf the official pastime of affluent macho yuppies. Nevertheless, when you are jabbering on your cell phone during a round of golf, you are cheating yourself of a proper, focused round. You are also cheating your business affairs by conversing while distracted by a round of golf. The inherent guilt over having conflicted purposes is evidenced by common verbiage like "sneak out of the office for a round of golf."

This lack of clarity leads to a scattered approach to life. When you try to be in two places at once—for example, making the golf course or playground swings your mobile office—you are not able to be truly present for either. Attempting to bite off more than you can chew, trying to achieve goals by the brute force of will, or ignoring emotional factors like flagging motivation levels can deplete your most important natural resources, such as a positive attitude and love for the activity you're engaged in.

WHEN YOU TRY TO BE IN TWO PLACES AT ONCE . . . YOU ARE NOT ABLE TO BE TRULY PRESENT FOR EITHER.

Actually, we might rephrase this success factor as clarity of a *good* purpose. Many people are pretty clear about a purpose of making money and boosting their self-esteem through achievement and the accumulation of more and more stuff. What many are unclear about, however, is who they are and what lies beyond the dangling carrot they are obsessed with chasing. Does it interest you to lead a healthy, balanced, happy life? Or is it enough to just win without enjoying the process or respecting your health? Lance's commentary from the eyes of a cancer survivor is only an opinion, but it's certainly one worth reflecting upon. You don't necessarily need dramatic elements like a life-threatening illness to evolve your perspective. By reflecting on your past life experience, and the words and lessons of others, you can gain the inspiration you need to change your life at any time.

The Chemotivator

Bob Babbitt of *Competitor* magazine believes that Lance's cancer experience was a powerful catalyst for his developing the clarity of purpose and focus that he did not have in his early days as an athlete.

BODY BY LANCE

It's been reported that Lance's body weight during his Tour de France reign fluctuated between 175 pounds in the off- or early season down to a superlean 162 pounds at the Tour starting line. The latter was below his natural set point and required great effort and discipline to reach. Because there is a thin line between peak form and overtraining, burnout, or depletion, Lance could maintain that weight only for a single month every year.

In contrast, many athletes race year-round and always maintain satisfactory fitness levels. They gain comfort and security from the fact that they can always step out the door and turn in a decent race result. Therefore, they are always watching their weight, caloric intake, and hours of sleep and have moods that are dictated by the quality of their most recent workouts. They never let go of their security blanket of being a competitive athlete because subconsciously they know that they never really make the ultimate sacrifice for peak performance. This might involve making deeper commitments during the peak competitive season and consequently allowing themselves to enjoy a true off-season—a mental and physical break from the pressure and tension involved in an intense athletic pursuit. Here they would obey one of the fundamental laws of nature, that only when the body rests from the stress of physical exercise does it have a chance to adapt and grow stronger.

"When Lance got cancer, he realized that he had to focus everything he had to beat the disease and save his life. He had to learn about the treatment process, the chemo drugs, and all the medical science. All of a sudden he became a serious and totally focused student fighting for his life. When he recovered, that mentality transferred over to cycling. The cancer experience changed him from head to toe. It allowed him to build a physique and a mentality ideally suited for the Tour, and he became the most focused rider in the sport."

Here we can learn a valuable lesson, for as Babbitt reminds us, "We all struggle in the area of focus. Even motivated people see opportunities coming from so many different directions that it diverts their attention. The average person is juggling a family, job, hobbies, extended family, and everything else that they are faced with in daily life. When people are not focused, they make excuses beforehand to protect themselves from the pain of failure, and that becomes a vicious cycle. I remember being at the Olympic triathlon venue in Sydney in 2000, watching the team mechanics work on the athletes' bicycles the day before the race. Noticing one particularly filthy bike, I correctly guessed who it belonged to. The mechanic was surprised that I could peg that athlete out of all the possible choices, but it was totally fitting to that person's character that he would be so unprepared as to schlep a dirty bike to the Olympics!

"Lance is an amazing multitasker, but he was completely focused on a single goal of winning the Tour de France," Babbitt observes. "He never lost sight of the fact that everything around him required that he win the Tour. I believe that he dealt with that kind of pressure by staying focused or even strengthening his focus. In contrast, most people have trouble dealing with pressure, and it typically causes them to lose focus. In 2003 Lance really struggled in the Tour, but he was still able to win—barely—while not at his best. I think that scared the hell out of him. He realized how lucky he was to win and how easily it could slip away. He made the comment after the race that he was going to have to get more 'monkish' for the next year. So he intensified his focus, eliminated distractions, and what happened in 2004? He obliterated the field."

When someone has a clarity of purpose that powerful, it can be intimidating to opponents. "The spectacle of Lance's dominance is interesting," says Babbitt. "He—and other legends, like triathlete

Mark Allen—develop this veil of invincibility such that the other athletes believe they are racing for second place. Look what happened in the first time trial of the 2005 Tour. When Lance passed Jan Ullrich [surprisingly making up a one-minute stagger between their start times over the extremely short racing distance of nineteen kilometers, or about twelve miles], the Tour was over. After that, everyone was racing for second place."

Having Your Cake and Eating It, Too

Lance's clear purpose and deep, evolved sources of motivation enabled him to rise above the pitfalls of the ego and fragile motivation. A person who is motivated by money or glory or to satisfy ego or compulsion is vulnerable to fear, anxiety, and disappointment when arbitrary measurable results are not attained. The tendency to force things to happen on an unnatural timeline inevitably has negative consequences. It doesn't matter if you are pursuing a mate, a college degree, a big sales deal, or a finish line—superficial motivators can throw you for a loop and result in diminished motivation and performance. Many people can't handle success, because once they get there, they get caught up in the excess and lose their motivation and focus. Many people can't handle failure, because self-worth is intertwined with performance. Failure in this circumstance breeds more failure.

Someone with a clear purpose and motivated by love of the journey derives rewards that transcend the fickle winning and losing of the superficial world. The feeling of satisfaction from giving a maximum effort is priceless. An athlete, a business executive, or a college student who can see beyond tangible results taps into an incredible treasure trove of energy, motivation, and confidence. Lao-tzu said, "A good traveler has no fixed plans and is not intent on arriving." This is a nice concept, great for Mr. Tzu and his frequent-flier account. Approaching your athletic or work career with the mind-set that the journey is emphasized over the end result can be

THE COMEBACK BEGINS

Bob Babbitt recalls a defining point in Lance's career at the very first race he contested after his cancer hiatus—the 1998 Ride for the Roses in his hometown of Austin. In the multilap criterium-style bike race for an invited field of professionals, it was believed that Lance would ride a few ceremonial laps with the field (bike races often start with such ceremonial processions, where the field agrees not to begin serious racing until a specified time later in the race) and then drop out and observe the real racing.

Babbitt was the race announcer for the event. "The race was one hundred laps—fifty miles—through the streets of downtown Austin. After ten laps [the expected drop point for Lance], he continues on with the field. He's there for twenty laps, thirty, sixty—still going strong. They get to the final lap, and it's he and Chann McRae [a childhood friend of Lance's from Plano, Texas, who improbably also went on to a distinguished professional cycling career—including a U.S. pro championship] ahead of the field. Lance drops Chann and crosses the line alone with the hometown crowd going crazy. To me, that moment was it. That's when Lance got a taste of how much he missed racing and how much he loved winning. From that point on, I considered him back. When I heard him announce his intentions for the 1999 Tour de France, I started telling people that he was going to win."

very difficult to implement, however. There is a tremendous necessity in the modern world to achieve measurable goals—quarterly earnings estimates for the corporation, finish times and places for the athlete, grades for the student. It might not fly if Joe College tells Mom and Dad, "It's all about the journey," while he languishes for six years at State U with cool friends and poor grades.

The trick is to blend and balance a devotion to more evolved forms of motivation and definition of purpose with a commitment to achieve measurable goals. It's OK to focus on and strive for victory, as long as you appreciate the importance and value of the journey. It is with this stance that you hone your confidence, your motivation, and an unshakable positive attitude. Lance's multiple Tour de France victories are a product of total devotion to peak performance. His ability to peak at the perfect time is unsurpassed in the history of sports. Practically speaking, this was a product of a careful progression of workload and planned downtime to experience continued improvement and minimize risk of overtraining, injury, or illness. This day-to-day devotion and sacrifice for a distant goal was possible only because he loved every single step in the process.

IT'S OK TO FOCUS ON AND STRIVE FOR VICTORY, AS LONG AS YOU APPRECIATE THE IMPORTANCE AND VALUE OF THE JOURNEY.

Finding Your Own Clarity

An amusing and oft-repeated quote from Lance that conveys the depth of his commitment was that he began to prepare for his next Tour de France the day after his previous victory. Rip Esselstyn is a healthy-eating enthusiast who has been lauded by national media for converting firefighters at his Austin station from traditional Texas fried flesh fare to a vegetarian diet. He remembers a telling e-mail he received in August of 2003. "It's only a few days after I watched Lance win—but struggle—at the Tour," he recalls. The e-mail read, "Rip—L.A. here. I'm ready to get serious about my diet. Put me on a program."

Fat and Foibles

On the other hand is the disposition of Lance's perennial main rival, Ullrich. "Discipline and ambition are important, but not for the whole year," Ullrich explained in a 2004 interview published on Cyclingnews.com. Ullrich has had a well-publicized and criticized penchant for adding too many extra pounds in the off-season, hampering his progression to peak condition when the critical spring-training period comes around. Other off-season highlights on Ullrich's résumé include a doping suspension for ingesting the recreational drug Ecstasy, crashing his Porsche (into a bike rack, believe it or not) while driving intoxicated, and being evicted from the 2006 Tour as part of a large doping scandal. Martin Dugard theorizes, quite perceptively, that Ullrich's off-season habits may be a rebellion from his East Germany sports machine roots, where his childhood and personal freedom were swapped for a chance to glorify the state with an Olympic cycling medal. "Cycle racing stole my youth," states Jens Voight, another top professional, who developed in the same East German sporting academy as Ullrich.

Echoing Freud, motivational guru Tony Robbins says that everything we do is motivated by either the pursuit of pleasure or to avoid pain. Everyone needs to seek pleasure, happiness, stress release, and peace of mind. For Ullrich, the rigors of a phenomenally difficult physical job have been balanced by a less-restricted diet and lifestyle in the off-season. Ullrich claims that it's important to stay true to one's basic nature, to be happy and balanced in life while pursuing an awesome competitive goal. As he told Cyclingnews.com, "The people that are important to me trust me and don't try to change me, which would be impossible anyway. I have to go my own way. I can't be everything, that's just how I am. Some say that we Rostockers [Rostock is the region of the former East Germany that Ullrich hails from] have an elephant skin. That helps sometimes."

At first glance, we might scoff at his story as a rationalization for being beaten by an opponent who was more focused and better prepared. However, these insights come from a Tour de France champion (and five-time runner-up with a third-place and fourth-place finish as well), Olympic gold medalist, and one of the greatest cyclists in history. Were it not for Lance having a proximate birth date and career span, we would be talking about *the* greatest cyclist in history.

What would have happened had Ullrich watched his diet, kept the winter pounds off, been more disciplined in training—been more like Lance? The knee-jerk response is to say that he might have beaten Lance or certainly been closer to him. However, upon further reflection, someone departing from his or her intuition and basic nature is going to struggle. It's likely that Ullrich would have come up injured or burned out in an attempt to mirror Lance's approach and temperament. Ullrich has clarity of purpose and trusts deeply in his own approach. It is telling to observe that even in the face of "evidence" in the form of repeated beatings by Lance, Ullrich resisted the temptation to mirror Lance's approach in attempting to beat him.

Junk Food and Spreadsheets

When I witnessed Lance once chow down some junk food cookies and diet soda from the minibar on his private jet (I wonder if he was charged extra), I mentioned the disconnect between someone who has Bart Knaggs designing spreadsheets to compare the relative performance of race wheels (factoring aerodynamic performance values with weight in grams) and fueling the machine that will propel those wheels with toxic crap. Obviously, Lance believed that enjoying a couple of cookies and a soda of no nutritional value during the off-season was not a big deal. He easily could have become obsessed with his diet, hired an organic macrobiotic vegetarian chef to prepare his meals for him, and adopted the belief that he was enjoying a significant advantage over his competitors by virtue of a superclean and highly nutritious diet.

The difference in performance between Lance's top-ten race wheel prospects is infinitesimal by any reasonable measure. However, the feeling Lance got when he mounted his bike for competition—of knowing that he had done more homework and had better equipment (even if the difference was trivial) than his rivals—was priceless. Lance did what he needed to do to get his mind-set in the right place for peak performance. If he had instead commanded his team to junk the spreadsheets and choose the highest bidder for wheels, he could have developed a mind-set that his wheel choice among leading brands was inconsequential.

SOMEONE DEPARTING FROM HIS OR HER INTUITION AND BASIC NATURE IS GOING TO STRUGGLE.

"Lance did what he needed to do" is an important characterization, because Lance indeed was the one steering the ship for the duration of his career. In contrast, many athletes in team sports or under the influences of domineering coaches are forced to do what tradition or the system believe to be important. If someone had enforced strict dietary guidelines on Lance that he was not happy about or congruent with, it would not have been a successful venture—even if he improved the nutrient quality of his diet.

Some athletes gain energy and strength from a more relaxed approach to competition. The people who criticized Michael Jordan for staying out till the wee hours gambling in casinos during the NBA Finals series fail to understand the power of an athlete who is true to his basic nature. Jordan and other champions (who, in contrast, might be religious about getting to bed early before games) are intuitive enough to understand exactly what lifestyle factors, attitude, and behavior they need in order to achieve peak performance. A smart coach or team would cook up green eggs and ham without a second thought if the star athlete felt they made him perform at his best.

It's not as easy as just blindly mirroring the approach of some-one who has been successful. As Mark Sisson said about business, "If it were easy, then everyone would be doing it." Human beings are not robots; they do not like to be deprived of their free will. Everyone has to find their own way, their own purpose, and live in accordance with that. If you can be clear about your purpose and understand your shortcomings and the reality that there can be only one CEO or Tour de France winner, you have a fighting shot at happiness and fulfillment. When you pursue a goal with clarity of purpose, you have to be true to your basic nature, the highest expression of your talents, and the reality of your life circumstances.

"IF IT WERE EASY, THEN EVERYONE WOULD BE DOING IT."

—Mark Sisson

To live the lie of striving for goals that are unrealistic or impossible or of talking out of one side of your mouth ("I'll do whatever it takes to get to the top—working weekends, whatever") and acting counter to that ("Uh, except this weekend—I got a bachelor party in Vegas, baby!") will break your spirit and lead to nothing but frustration, envy, and other deadly sins. Sadly, double-talk is what many of us are doing. I have coached many highly motivated, goal-oriented, type A, supersuccessful people with a passion for triathlon—people who are willing to do whatever it takes to excel. Nevertheless, there seems to be a widespread struggle with the most basic elements of pursuing peak performance, like moderating the pull of ego demands to treat the body with respect, balancing stress and rest in both life and training, and delaying instant gratification in favor of sensible progression to long-term goals. They think they are committed to excellence, but their desire to beat somebody to the top of the next hill overpowers a pure and effective long-term approach.

The Checkered Flag

Whatever your goal, you will gain more enjoyment and self-satisfaction when you have clarity of purpose. If your goal is daunting, such as winning the Tour de France, it will certainly consume your life and require tremendous sacrifices. You can also have powerful and compelling goals like raising a happy family; being a good schoolteacher, nurse, or accountant; and leading a healthy and balanced lifestyle. In these cases, your "sacrifices" might be to turn off that competitive faucet when tempted to go overboard with a fitness or material pursuit—the opposite of the sacrifices made by a champion athlete or corporate superstar.

In the case of a friend of mine who drives race cars for a living, he and his wife both applied clarity of purpose to allow him to enjoy uninterrupted sleep in a separate room for the duration of his children's infancy. Sure, he had to sacrifice the joy of coparenting a crying infant in the middle of the night, but he and his wife were also less inclined than the next couple to have him show up to work a little groggy. The significance of missing some sleep tends to magnify while driving at speeds exceeding two hundred miles per hour.

Your peak performance endeavors may have little in common with Lance's or a professional race car driver's, but the insights still apply. Deal with reality like a champion, and put your unrealistic dreams to bed with a clear conscience. Understand that peak performance in any endeavor requires a healthy mind, body, and spirit—and take steps to put your well-being ahead of the intense pace and competitive frenzy of the rat race. Lance's example of carefully moderating his caloric intake to attain the optimal body fat levels for the Tour, strange as it may seem, has some relevance to the two-thirds of Americans classified as overweight and the one-third of those classified as clinically obese. It's worth considering whether our collective eating habits are worth the massive pain caused by diet-related health problems, fitness limitations, and premature deaths that result.

Some reading this book may be stuck in the wrong job or wrong relationship or may be otherwise performing below potential and suffering because of it. We are all deserving of the clarity to push forward and expand our capabilities, regardless of what direction they take us. For me, in 1995, it meant stepping off the professional triathlon circuit and into a new career, sitting on my butt in an office. This career change was a definitive step forward for me, despite the fact that it was far less glamorous than jetting around the globe trying to achieve glory in triathlons. For others, it may mean jumping off the corporate ladder to a soft landing of a less stressful job and more balanced life.

The closing message of Dugard's *Chasing Lance* reads, "What my pursuit of Lance had shown me was that life was to be lived to its fullest; that daily process of pushing forward, always forward, constantly exploring and expanding one's capabilities, was the great mandate." With your mandate in hand, don't get consumed by the pull of the ego and the rat race and overlook the fact that you are the one who should define your playing field. The parent who tends to the crying baby at night with love and patience is just as much a champion as someone who crosses the finish line amid thousands of cheering fans.

STEPS TO DEVELOP SUCCESS FACTOR 2: CLARITY OF PURPOSE

1. **Do what you love.** The most powerful motivator of all is love of the activity. Look beyond the pressures and expectations of the rat race, and pursue goals that give you the most internal satisfaction, regardless of outcome. This will prevent you from falling

into the dangerous trap of superficial motivations (money, glory, or to satisfy ego or compulsion), which bring disappointment and diminished self-esteem when arbitrary measurable results are not attained.

2. Find your own clarity. Choose healthy goals that are aligned with your basic nature, the highest expression of your talents, and the reality of your life circumstances. Then pursue them in a way that makes you happy, nourishes your spirit, and will leave no regrets in the future. You can't blindly copy someone else's approach and expect to enjoy it or to end up with the same results.

3. Appreciate competition. It's OK to be an intense competitor and have a strong desire for victory, provided you do not attach self-esteem to outcome. Rather than stress over results, draw strength from doing what you love, and focus only on giving your best effort. Fight hard in battle, but be sure to go enjoy some ice cream afterward. Understand that defeat can teach valuable lessons that help you improve in the future.

4. Eliminate guilt. Take decisive action in your life and don't look back, divert your attention, or try to bite off more than you can chew. Feeling guilty is a little game we play with ourselves to give permission to avoid something or repeat the same behavior. Deal with your reality like a champion instead of living in frustration for what you don't have or can't do. Constantly explore and expand your capabilities, as Dugard suggests, instead of making excuses for areas where you fall short.

5. Be patient. Resist the temptation of the ego and instant gratification in favor of a sincere commitment to long-term goals. Have the patience to improve at a natural rate rather than forcing things to happen because of harmful influences like the performances and expectations of others.

Courtesy of Trek Bicycle Corporation/Photographer Nicole Cook

6

SUCCESS FACTOR 3
SPECIALIZED INTELLIGENCE

Lance exhibited a highly specialized and refined form of intelligence perfectly suited to his cycling career. Specialized intelligence for cycling or any other specific endeavor is not necessarily directly relevant to general intelligence as measured by IQ, but it sure doesn't hurt to apply high intellectual ability to specialized goals. "Lance has a very deep intelligence and an incredible memory," Bill Stapleton says. "He can sit down with any CEO, and if he learns something about a company, he remembers it. The sponsors and others he does business with always remark, 'Hey, that guy is really smart.' It's something people don't assume because he didn't go to college and also because most athletes are not Rhodes scholars."

As we have learned from Lance's transformation from impetuous, aggressive one-day racer (occasionally losing to weaker riders due to strategic errors) to master strategist of the three-week Tour de France, his intellect came into play even in the seemingly straightforward challenge of applying more raw physical power to the pedals than his rivals. This is not just because strategy and teamwork are critical in cycling. Even in a straightforward, individual competition like a long-distance running race, you still have to be very intelligent to win.

The fastest way to run a race is to maintain the same speed (assuming a flat course and consistent conditions) throughout. This is proved by an examination of the split times of top performances like Deena Kastor's American record in the marathon (set at the 2006 London Marathon) of two hours, nineteen minutes, thirty-six seconds. She hit the halfway point (13.1 miles) on the course at 1:09.48 and then covered the second half in the same time! Her split times at five-kilometer checkpoints along the course read 16:32, 16:37, 16:32, 16:31, 16:24, 16:32, 16:35, and so on. To an observer that day (especially one not interested in marathon running), the effort may have appeared robotic and unexciting. However, the ability to properly disperse energy to maintain a steady pace in the face of ever-increasing fatigue (Kastor's first miles were quite comfortable, while the final miles were excruciating) requires tremendous intelligence, patience, and intuition. This is true not only for the race itself but in training properly for peak performance.

We all face an endless succession of challenges and decisions that determine whether we succeed or struggle. Specialized intelligence—for competitive sports, relationships, career, leadership, and so on—is critical to making the right decisions, to habitually placing yourself in the right place at the right time so as to have unwavering good luck, to constantly observing where you stand in the big picture and knowing where to head, and to avoiding temptations of the ego and the distractions that disrupt focus on long-term goals.

The Bear Trap

"Cancer awakened Lance to the fact that he was intelligent," remembers Bart Knaggs. "Prior to that, his head was something stuck between his shoulders that got in the way when he put his shirt on. His precancer athletic career was a testament to brute strength and aggression. He'd just go out and ride hard, but not really paying attention to proper training principles. His diet was for shit, he weighed 175 pounds, and his day-to-day commitment wavered. Everyone was telling him he was the greatest—'Hey, you're world champion at the age of twenty-one!' There was no reason to dig deeper or cultivate an intelligent approach; it wasn't really his thing."

Knaggs continues, "It's no wonder Lance was this way, with our narrow definition of *intelligence* in society and our destructive tendency to label people, even when they are just kids. Lance didn't thrive in the structured, rote educational system, nor was there a rich traditional education influence in his home. He essentially got the message that he was dumb. So he naturally played to his strengths and denied his weaknesses by becoming a superathlete. That's fine until you get to the elite level of professional athletics, where everyone brings physical strength to the table.

"When he was diagnosed, he called me up and I said, 'Holy shit! We have to do something.' I jumped on the Internet and accumulated stacks of research, but back in 1996 research and Internet resources were minimal. My former business partner, who was a testicular cancer survivor, advised Lance to understand and drive his own treatment. Particularly since he was an athlete with special considerations [common treatment drugs had side effects like causing potentially permanent lung damage or harming equilibrium, both problematic to a hopeful cycling comeback], he was forced to get involved.

"Lo and behold, guess what happened? He discovered that he had a huge faculty for numbers and science and that he had an absolute bear trap for a mind. Lance simply doesn't forget shit. He is also an obsessive and tremendously inquisitive type, so he absorbed the information that was presented like a sponge. His doctors became annoyed with us because we asked too many questions. I'd be like, 'What about that study from Amsterdam where the rats . . . ,' and the doctor would go, 'Jesus Christ! Where did you find that? What are you trying to do? You have to realize I went to medical school and have years of specialized training. . . .' It's not that Lance broke the code on cancer. Cancer broke the code on Lance. When he recovered, he had a new package: in addition to his lungs and legs, he had his brain," concludes Knaggs.

"IT'S NOT THAT LANCE BROKE THE CODE ON CANCER. CANCER BROKE THE CODE ON LANCE."

—Bart Knaggs

Follow the Leader

One of Lance's greatest and perhaps least-celebrated legacies was his ability to motivate, inspire, and lead his team and his entire organization in the quest for the Tour de France title. The volume of books, articles, and seminars about leadership techniques attest that this is an extremely elusive skill to cultivate, requiring tremendous intellect and emotional sensitivity.

Dan Osipow, who served as the team's media-communications director for all seven of Lance's Tour wins, remembers how Lance's mentality affected the entire organization. "Lance is a leader like none other," Osipow told me. "Since Lance was focused on winning, that became the mission for everyone involved. In Europe the Tour de France is such a big deal that merely finishing is a tremendous accomplishment. You go back to your village a big hero. Thus many riders were completely satisfied just to finish the race, and many teams were content simply to contest the single-day stage wins. The atmosphere on our team was completely different. Going to the Tour knowing we could win created a tremendous expectation and pressure to perform—whether you were a rider or mechanic or whatever. Because of the dynamics of racing for the overall victory and protecting time advantages, every guy on Lance's team knew they were going to be called upon for twenty-one days in a row.

"Lance's competitive intensity and focus were infectious," Osipow continues. "Nothing was left to chance with his approach and thus the team's approach. Lance's attitude was, 'If I'm going to get beat by a better rider, I'm going to get beat. But I will not get beat by not doing everything possible in my power to gain an advantage.' As a consequence of this intelligent approach, Lance created a ton of good luck for himself. People scratch their heads, wondering how he got out of so many jams. But if you examine the entire approach—the incredible bond Lance had with [team director] Johan Bruyneel, the annual previewing of all the routes, the total focus of the team on a single goal—it's easy to see how he created his own good luck." Or as Martin Dugard wrote in *Chasing Lance* about American Dave Zabriskie's one-bike crash just before the finish of stage four while wearing the yellow jersey in 2005, "Funny how some guys always find a way to crash and some guys always find a way to win."

In the Tour de France, where the individual winner receives all of the glory and most of the financial rewards, it's not an easy thing to inspire a team of people to sacrifice their personal ambitions for a singular cause. Coming from basically zero experience (remember that before cycling, Lance was a triathlete, which is a completely individual sport) or formal training, Lance became one of the greatest leaders ever in sports. He displayed tremendous intelligence in understanding his role at the center of his team and the entire sport and how to effectively deal with this intense pressure.

"Besides modernizing the sport technologically, with the use of the wind tunnel and equipment innovations, Lance modernized the concept of leadership in cycling," Stapleton observes. "European bike teams simply do not have the team cohesiveness we are familiar with in an American football team. Because riders switch teams so often in a total free-agent system, they mainly look out for themselves. Lance established an organization where he was the clear leader and the team members were committed to a single, clearly established goal. He did this by taking care of the riders—sticking with them through bad results, working for them in the spring [to help them win races during Lance's Tour de France preparation period when he deemphasized his own results], and offering his teammates incentive to share in the upside of his victory. He became a leader that people really wanted to work for," explains Stapleton.

From Lance's commentary on leadership, it's evident that he leads by action rather than the more common method of blowhard commentary, posturing, rhetoric, and intimidation. "I don't think the leader should ever stand up and say why they're a leader. That would be questionable to me," he states. "When you are trying to lead a team and you have to have all these characteristics to motivate them and keep them going . . . it would probably be more interesting and meaningful to ask the other members of the team what makes me a leader." I asked Lance if it was difficult to face the pressure that comes from a multimillion-dollar enterprise with dozens of employees depending on his winning the Tour. "No, it was never difficult, because during my career I was able to do the work at a high level. That gave me the confidence to know that things should work out OK."

This is a phenomenal outlook for a high-profile athlete to have. People want to work for someone who is a champion in every sense of the word. Beyond just crossing the finish line first, Lance created a positive, winning environment where riders had fun training and racing on the team but at the same time were committed in every way to peak performance. It was the same on the sponsor's photo shoot—laughing and joking with the crew while at the same time keeping everyone totally focused and running on hyperspeed efficiency. At the Tour, the pressure was inherent in the magnitude of the goal, but thanks to Lance's positive and evolved outlook, the pressure served only to rally the troops, not paralyze them with fear. I asked Lance about whether he ever got nervous or anxious before a race. "Sure," he replied. "I think some prerace jitters are healthy and normal. Especially early in the Tour or in a big one-day race like the Olympics or the World Championships. During the Tour, I typically felt less and less nervous as the race progressed. After an important stage, I felt more relaxed, particularly if I'd gained two minutes that I knew could never be taken away." I asked how that disposition rubbed off on his teammates. "My teammates definitely got more anxious and nervous," explained Lance. "They had a big job—there was a lot on the line for them. You can't win the Tour without a team, and I had to try and be a calming influence. This required some effort before the critical days of the race, but after that, it's pretty straightforward."

THANKS TO LANCE'S POSITIVE AND EVOLVED OUTLOOK, THE PRESSURE SERVED ONLY TO RALLY THE TROOPS, NOT PARALYZE THEM WITH FEAR.

I don't blame you if you require an interpreter to decipher Lance's statements. Being relaxed under pressure may seem natural to Lance but highly unlikely for most other humans placed in his position. Lance seemed to be more cognizant of the pressure his teammates faced than the exponentially greater pressure he faced as the race favorite.

Clearly, it's not normal for a race favorite to become more relaxed as a race progresses—that's backward. Anyone can relate to the escalation of pressure as the stakes increase. It's a daunting battle to clear out fearful, anxious emotions and remain calm. In Lance's case, with a scale a hundred times greater than most of us have ever faced or even imagined, he seems oblivious to pressure, tension, or anxiety— even right on the cusp of realizing the victory that he has focused intently on for the entire year.

The Luck of the Patient and Well Prepared

Daniel Coyle's *Lance Armstrong's War* contains an account of how Spanish rider Iban Mayo displayed tremendous form and dominated Lance in 2004 pre-Tour competitions, causing great consternation to Armstrong and his advisers. Rather than panic or lose motivation, however, Lance stayed his course and continued with his methodical preparation. He and his crew were left to speculate that if Mayo maintained his world-beating form, he could quite possibly take Lance down in the Tour. They also speculated that it could be extremely difficult for Mayo to straddle that thin line between dominant peak performance and exhaustion, injury, and burnout. Indeed, Mayo was fried by the time July came around and didn't offer the slightest challenge to Lance in France.

It takes a tremendous amount of restraint and patience to smoothly progress with your studies, career, or athletic goals. The natural human tendency to pursue instant gratification and ego reinforcement must be eliminated in favor of total devotion to a long-term goal. The demands of the ego must be ignored to the extent that suppressing one's competitive instinct in favor of patient progress toward a long-term goal, or getting soundly whipped by an opponent, is not the slightest bit disruptive to the focus on long-term goals. Believe me, 99.9 percent of all athletes, even accomplished professionals, screw this up.

When you think of Lance's face on TV during the Tour, in full-scale, relentless attack over his helpless opponents, you may want to remember where that same face often was a few months prior to the Tour. While others rode to glory in anonymous races like Semana Catalana or Tour of Murcia, Lance was in the middle of the pack, working for teammates and paying his dues to prepare for future conquests. He was still in control of his game—just in a different way.

THE NATURAL HUMAN TENDENCY TO PURSUE INSTANT GRATIFICATION AND EGO REINFORCEMENT MUST BE ELIMINATED IN FAVOR OF TOTAL DEVOTION TO A LONG-TERM GOAL.

For example, if Lance finished a February race ten minutes behind when he'd expected to be only six minutes behind, he simply used the information to adjust his future preparation and hit the next fitness checkpoint with more accuracy. On the flip side, when Lance surprisingly dominated the April 2004 Tour of Georgia, he offered a curious quote to the media: "I'm way ahead of my preparation from last year, which is not necessarily a good thing." Rather than becoming intoxicated by a surprisingly good result and accelerated fitness progress, Lance went back, huddled with his coaches, and adjusted his future training to ensure that he didn't peak too early for the Tour.

I pressed to determine whether Lance was ruffled just a little by getting his hat handed to him in early-season races. "No. I understand how it works. You can't be in super form all the time. You have to be patient with the natural progression of fitness. For example, I know that early in the season is a time for real suffering and readapting to a heavy workload. I was definitely comfortable getting beaten in the spring. The only important thing was to get fitter and stronger through February, March, April, May, and June to prepare for the Tour in July. I was always lucky with this progression."

A keen observer of the wonderful Nike-produced DVD *Road to Paris*, which followed Lance backstage as he and his team trained for the 2001 Tour de France, will note a telling comment from Lance that occurred during a team pep talk. With the riders dressed for battle and gathered in the team bus before the start of the four-day Circuit de la Sarthe stage race in April in northern France, team director Johan Bruyneel inspired the troops by saying, "Everyone here can win the Circuit de la Sarthe; everyone has the ability to . . ." At which point he was interrupted by a wisecrack from Lance, ". . . except me." Not the kind of statement you would expect from one of the most intense competitors ever seen in sport, but understandable when you see the big picture of Lance's career and clear purpose to peak for the Tour de France.

One of the ingredients of a champion athlete is a precise, focused training program. But the error most athletes make is failing to understand and face their biggest enemy—themselves. Often the specific objective of a training session gets junked as soon as a training partner makes an aggressive move that the ego cannot resist. Consequently, many athletes leave their best efforts on the training road or in lesser races. The workplace analogy is clear, particularly with the new millennium trend of jumping ship every two years for a more alluring opportunity, an instant gratification play that often compromises long-term career development.

Developing the ability to suppress ego-driven instincts and accept defeat and criticism as a natural consequence of steady preparation for a future peak effort is a priceless talent. People striving for success often will discipline, measure, and control everything in their lives to a ridiculous extent, but they will fail again and again to discipline the mind with an intelligent approach. They can spend months preparing carefully for a peak performance only to get psyched out on the starting line and irrationally depart from their strategy.

Developing Specialized Intelligence

Let's discuss three key steps critical to developing specialized intelligence in your area of peak performance—work, athletic, or otherwise. These steps are assimilate past experience, cultivate intuition, and gain big-picture perspective about your endeavors.

Assimilate Past Experience

A champion like Lance is able to assimilate past experience, both success and failure, in a positive and empowering manner. In contrast, most of the general population live a life filled with repeated mistakes and have difficulty with behavior modification. The athlete has a learning forum so dramatic that it becomes a huge advantage and catalyst for positive change. You *must* learn from experience and adjust future behavior to survive as an athlete. In the real world, provided you're not a criminal, you can bounce through a whole lifetime of repeating mistakes over and over.

YOU *MUST* LEARN FROM EXPERIENCE AND ADJUST FUTURE BEHAVIOR TO SURVIVE AS AN ATHLETE.

If you drive too fast, spend more money than you make, talk with your mouth full, gossip behind people's backs, or overdramatize relationship conflicts, you carry these goodies around in your baggage for years, if not decades. In contrast, the boxer who telegraphs his left hook gets his nose bloodied. The pitcher who hangs his curve-

SPECIALIZED INTELLIGENCE ON THE CORPORATE LADDER

Martin Brauns commented on how specialized intelligence applies to the intensely competitive business world. "I think one has to be extremely driven—extremely competitive and hungry," according to Brauns. "I can't say that I embarked on my career thinking, 'Gee, in twenty years I'd like to be a CEO.' In fact, when I started my technology career in 1982, I was naive enough that I probably didn't even have a clear concept of what a CEO role even entailed. But what I did have was drive and a maniacal focus on graduating to the next level, on taking on the next higher rung of responsibility. Twelve or so years into my career, the goal of becoming a CEO began to take shape.

"I think there are two particular forms of specialized intelligence that serve well those who aspire to executive roles," Brauns continues. "First—and some might think this pedestrian—it is absolutely vital to hone your presentation and persuasion skills. Start, of course, by learning to listen. Through extensive practice you develop your active listening skills and then your persuasion and leadership skills. Second, you must assimilate and learn from your own mistakes.

"When I interview executive talent, I'm not necessarily looking for people who have had one smashing success after another—it's likely they were just serially lucky. I'm looking for people who have actually hit a few speed bumps in life or in their career. I ask a lot of questions about what they learned from those stumbles and discover whether they are a student of themselves. Have they been able to assimilate the lessons that life has served up, take responsibility for their own actions and reactions? And can they tell me how, if in the future they were confronted with a similar situation, they would handle it differently or better? Failure and hardship can teach invaluable lessons, if you're open and willing to assimilate them.

"Furthermore, I think great leaders and great human beings need to operate from an automatic, ingrained, inbred reflex to do the right thing, to be true to a personal moral code. One could call it a default setting that automatically dials up the chivalrous highest-road response in any situation, regardless of whether that high road is easy or convenient. It is possible to be a good sport and chivalrous while being intensely competitive—a gentleman warrior. It's also true that business, as well as life, is not fair. The character wearing the white hat doesn't always win. And sometimes those motivated by fear, low self-worth, and scarcity achieve success. However, I think someone with a strong foundation of character and positive attitude, who carries themselves well, will enjoy more success and be better able to handle setbacks. It's the core principles that drag you out of bed every morning more so than the desire to crush an opponent."

ball gets shelled and sent to the minors. The golfer who yips her short putts misses cuts and goes home from the tour. The naked shame of athletic failure motivates great athletes to change like chameleons and become ever more intelligent in response to environmental feedback.

Notice I said the *great* athletes. Most athletes, even at the professional level, ascend to their rightful spot on the ladder and stay there. They survive, but like the rest of us in the real world, they are saddled with the detrimental behavior patterns that prevent them from rising higher in their profession. They may not make blatant, embarrassing mistakes repeatedly, but neither do they achieve their ultimate potential. Perhaps they lack the intelligence to become aware of, analyze, and improve upon their weaknesses.

"IT'S THE CORE PRINCIPLES THAT DRAG YOU OUT OF BED EVERY MORNING MORE SO THAN THE DESIRE TO CRUSH AN OPPONENT."

—Martin Brauns

Phoenix Suns point guard Steve Nash, the two-time NBA Most Valuable Player for the 2004 to 2005 and 2005 to 2006 seasons, is a classic overachiever. Nash is an unimposing six-foot-two white guy from Canada, not especially fast, strong, or otherwise physically gifted—a rather uncommon skill set in the NBA. Nevertheless, he has ascended to the highest level of the sport with an awesome work ethic, competitive intensity, and superior "court sense" (another way of saying specialized intelligence to play the game of basketball). His late-night escapades in college involved opening up the school gym (with his own key) and shooting baskets. In a 2006 *Sports Illustrated* feature story, Nash commented on the phenomenon of even top professional athletes falling short of their potential: "Most guys somewhere along the line will meet an obstacle they aren't willing to clear—whether it's shooting or dribbling or something off the court, like girls or partying. They will not keep on going. I kept on going."

Most people are mature enough to respect that loud music damages future hearing, smoking will kill you, and drinking till you puke is not a pleasant experience. Yet only the most driven, focused, and intelligent in the population carry it to the next level, where awareness is constantly high and informed decisions that promote one's best interests are made at every juncture.

The first step is to heighten your awareness. The next time you go to the golf course, give a presentation, complete a day of work, or take care of the kids, take a few moments to reflect on your performance and even ask others for honest feedback. It sounds simple, but it's something that is generally neglected by most of us who are too busy to worry about peak performance. This does not have to be a complex endeavor with a fancy daily planner complete with journal blanks for all of Stephen Covey's seven successful habits. I found my workdays became far more productive when my first act was to make a numerical to-do list with items ranked in order of priority. The mere act of pondering and ranking my to-do items helped sharpen my focus about what I wanted to accomplish in a workday and how to get there. (This isn't applicable to Lance's life, however, as Lance's oncologist Craig Nichols once told *Sports Illustrated*: "Lance doesn't have a to-do list. Things just get done, right now.")

Having a positive attitude is also a tremendous help. To let your past empower you instead of scar you, it is necessary to draw positive conclusions, even from failure and disappointment, and let go of any and all negativity. Lance has mentioned many times how cancer was the best thing that ever happened to him, because it changed his perspective, made him a more disciplined athlete, gave him a greater appreciation for life, and so on. "If there is a purpose to the suffering that is cancer, I think it must be this: It's meant to improve us," he wrote in *It's Not About the Bike*.

"LANCE DOESN'T HAVE A TO-DO LIST. THINGS JUST GET DONE, RIGHT NOW."

—Craig Nichols

Finally, adopting a defensive posture will help you assimilate past experience. This is a mind-set that not coincidentally is endemic to both cancer treatment and bike racing. In the Tour de France, Lance's goal was to assume the yellow jersey by completing individual time trials in less time and breaking away on mountain climbs. Once in the lead, the leader and his entire team have the strategy to protect the jersey from attacks by other riders and of course extend their advantage whenever possible. Hence, you would always see Lance and his teammates near the front of the field, vigilant against an opponent's attempt to break away from the pack and gain time.

Consequently, Lance seemed to comment in the defensive voice—about not wanting to lose the Tour—more often than expressing positive sentiments of wanting to win. This mentality might be problematic in other sports like tennis or golf, where a defensive posture can lead to tentative play and choking, but in cycling this is probably a good mentality to have. After all, the times that Lance went on the offensive and attacked in the sum total of all his Tours de France, where total riding time amounted to hundreds of hours, could be measured in mere minutes.

With a defensive, protective mind-set, you strive to avoid weakness and vulnerability against opponents. A company that has lost market share by not advertising in Spanish-language media will jump on board in order to defend against competitors looking to expose this weakness. A parent who sees her kid fall off the swing at the playground will stand closer on the next go-round, ready at a moment's notice to prevent a future accident.

Cultivate Intuition

In athletics modern theories of training and competitive strategy are extremely sophisticated and supported by extensive scientific study. Similarly, the business world places great importance on corporate structure, management techniques, sales and marketing strategies, and the like. Lance and his advisers invested tremendous time and energy researching and testing different training programs and formulas that enabled his body to attain ever-higher fitness levels. Factors like periodization (dividing the calendar year into periods characterized by different types of training), heart-rate training zones, exercise volumes and intensity, physical adaptations, and recovery rates were measured, applied, and modified throughout his career. This occurred on a daily basis in an effort to get the absolute top production out of his body and gain an edge over the competition.

Taking a step back and examining the bigger picture, it's apparent that while structure and scientifically proven training principles are crucial, there is something of equal or more importance—the dynamic, personal, emotional component of peak performance. Even the most disciplined and structured athlete like Lance is a human being with feelings and frailties that impact training decisions and fitness progress. I define intuition as a blend of instinct; critical thinking and reasoning; common sense; an awareness of one's mental, physical, and emotional states; and an ability to see the big picture of life and peak performance goals. Intuition is the inner voice that always knows the right thing to do. Should I date/marry this person? Should I move to this city and take this new job? Should I complete the proposed training plan today? Should I attempt to break from the pack here or wait until later?

In the modern world, intuition often gets snuffed out by insecurity, extreme emotional reactions, ego demands, obsessive-compulsive behavior, time deadlines, and the high-stress nature of the rat race. Cultivating intuition involves stepping back, slowing down, and listening to that inner voice at all costs. This requires a huge sacrifice, for the interrupting factors just described are very real and potentially monstrous in their influence.

A simple example for a highly motivated competitive athlete is a sore throat. The most sensible and prosperous long-term decision is to cease exercise until symptoms of declining health have stabilized. It's a proven fact that not only can you not build fitness when suffering from even a minor illness, but you can actually get worse with further exercise. Lance Armstrong did not win the Tour de France seven times by abusing his body with vigorous exercise in the presence of illness or injury. However, many athletes don't have the intelligence or the confidence to listen to their intuition and back off. Instead, compulsion, ego, and unrefined competitive instincts cause them to push on, digging themselves into a hole in the process.

In other worlds, such as parenting or in one's career, intuition can get snuffed out for similarly disappointing reasons. Devoted parents have a terrific intuition for child care—they sense when kids need rest, a snack, discipline, or comforting. On occasion, outside influences like peer pressure can lead a parent to act against her intuition. The result is often a meltdown or a kid picking up a cold from being pushed too hard or kept up too late when already tired. Looking back, we can typically identify when we gave up our own inner voices and submitted to the pressures of the world. Accumulating experiences like these gives us more knowledge and resolve to stay true to intuition in the future. It's not easy with the tempting Faustian bargain available in today's rat race. Like a developer of a residential subdivision, you can sell off chunks of your balanced life (time for family, exercise and other personal diversions, adequate sleep and restoration) for an increase in salary, a corner office, and a shiny new BlackBerry.

The reason humans dominate the planet over our physically stronger friends in the animal kingdom is that we have the ability to reason—to use intuitive powers to avoid danger, to say and do the appropriate things. If an animal is hungry and sees some food with a net hanging over it, the animal will lunge for the food and get entangled in the trap. The hungry human will see the food and the net, assess the risk versus reward of going for the food, and then intuitively take a pass on the food. Someone who lacks intuition, however, will keep reaching for the food and end up tangled in the figurative net of failure and repeated mistakes.

Gain Big-Picture Perspective

The third component of specialized intelligence is to have a complete understanding of all aspects of your endeavor, the elements required for peak performance and your role on a team or in an organization. Athletic competition, the business world, and most other endeavors are dynamic—every situation is different and requires a unique approach to succeed. Champions are intelligent enough to choose the route through the maze that leads to the cheese far more often than their competition.

SOMEONE WHO LACKS INTUITION, HOWEVER, WILL KEEP REACHING FOR THE FOOD AND END UP TANGLED IN THE FIGURATIVE NET OF FAILURE AND REPEATED MISTAKES.

Most of us are too busy keeping our heads down trying to get through the day to bother with an awareness of the big picture. But it's a form of retarded adolescence when one fails to consider the long-term consequences of current actions. Lance's case becomes even more problematic when you consider the difficulty in maintaining perspective as a celebrity and an international hero. The exponential escalation of pressure as he defended his Tour de France title year after year put his competitive career, not to mention his entire existence, under a high-powered microscope through which he could be viewed by millions around the world.

While Lance was able to maintain his lauded focus and healthy perspective, many other peak performers cannot. Believe it or not, even some of the world's top athletes have an upper threshold of their self-perception, beyond which they are not comfortable. They may be comfortable winning one world championship but not two or three. They may feel content to make millions of dollars ranking in the top ten but are unwilling to keep on going to contest the number one spot. When this is the case, they engage in subconscious self-sabotaging behavior to ensure the status quo and not introduce any uncomfortable elements or risks into their lives.

A great champion like Lance feels entirely comfortable with his place in the world, whether as the leader of a cycling team contending for the Tour de France title, a high-profile advocate for cancer research, or a celebrity. Shirking opportunity or obligations would make him feel uncomfortable, like when Michael Jordan couldn't bear *not* to have the ball in his hands at the end of the game. A champion understands the repercussions of celebrity and the inherent sacrifice required to ascend and remain at the very top of his or her profession. *Sacrifice* may not be the best word because the "sacrifices" they make in life to become champions feel natural and automatic. The gymnasts who win gold medals at fifteen are not lamenting missed prom dances and slumber parties, because they believe deeply and are totally focused on their destiny of becoming an Olympic champion.

Troy Hoidal remembers, "The second I met Lance, I knew he was a champion. Nothing has changed since our first meeting except the world now knows." While Lance is comfortable in the spotlight, he is at the same time able to separate self-esteem from performance and celebrity status. His statement "I consider myself a cancer survivor first" is an indication that his perspective is balanced and healthy. To approach sports from this stance frees him from pressure, tension, and anxiety, which are by-products of attaching self-esteem to performance. When you go to Hollywood and forget your roots, forget who you are, and get caught up in your character on the TV or movie screen, you become vulnerable to emotional stress and unhappiness in both success and failure.

> ## "WE MUST NOT FORGET TO INCLUDE LANCE'S DEFEATS AS PART OF WHAT BUILT HIS SOLID FOUNDATION OF SUCCESS."
> —Troy Hoidal

If you need to win to feel like a worthwhile human being, you are carrying some very heavy baggage up the mountains. When Bart Knaggs said, "Lots of guys *want* to win; Lance *has* to win," he was conveying Lance's competitive intensity accurately, but we must understand an important follow-up to this. If Lance had trained hard for the Tour de France and placed tenth, he would no doubt have been devastated, but he would have accepted the result (painfully) and moved on. He would have maintained his commitment to being a devoted athlete, father, son, cancer spokesperson, and businessman.

"We must not forget to include Lance's defeats as part of what built his solid foundation of success," Hoidal reminds us. If you lose sight of the big-picture perspective, the world will drag you down and you will have difficulty winning in the future. When you can respond to defeat with a positive attitude and intelligently implement the resultant lessons, you can continue to improve.

STEPS TO DEVELOP SUCCESS FACTOR 3: SPECIALIZED INTELLIGENCE

1. Be smart. Every peak performance endeavor, even something that is mostly physical and straightforward, requires an effective application of intellect. Ignoring the importance of an intelligent approach in favor of just working or training hard can often lead to getting psyched out or succumbing to pressure. Applying specialized intelligence means suppressing the ego, being patient, accepting defeat and criticism, and expertly handling the pressure that accompanies the pursuit of meaningful goals.

2. Assimilate past experience and failure. Heighten awareness of your approach and performance (in sports, work, parenting, or other endeavors). Maintain a positive attitude so that even failure and disappointment can empower you for the future. Adopt a defensive posture that will help you avoid future mistakes.

3. Cultivate intuition. Intuition is the little voice inside you that has the best sense of what to do—it is the dynamic, personal, emotional human component of peak performance. This is just as important as hitting the books, doing the miles, and proceeding with the straightforward, mechanical components of success. Make the commitment to avoid the traps of insecurity, extreme emotional reactions, ego demands, obsessive-compulsive behavior, time deadlines, and the high-stress, superficial demands of the rat race and instead to slow down and listen to your inner voice.

4. Adopt a big-picture perspective. Strive to understand all aspects of your peak performance endeavors, and be flexible to change your approach in response to competitive stimulation. Develop the ability to be an intense competitor, yet avoid attaching your happiness or self-esteem to the results. In this manner, you can become comfortable ascending to ever-higher levels of performance.

Graham Watson, grahamwatson.com

7

SUCCESS FACTOR 4
PURE CONFIDENCE

"Lance is not driven by fear of failure, like I think so many other athletes are," Bill Stapleton observes. "For example, on the morning of Luz Ardiden at the 2003 Tour, he was a little anxious, but he never seemed scared to me. He was just never afraid of losing."

The Luz Ardiden mountain stage near the end of the 2003 Tour was perhaps Lance's most vulnerable point at any of his seven Tour victories. It was the final week of the Tour, and two other riders (Jan Ullrich and Alexandre Vinokourov) were within eighteen seconds of him—the closest Tour in history that late in the event. The dramatic stage was highlighted by Lance's shocking crash (the strings of a child spectator's souvenir bag became entangled in his handlebars, instantly knocking him violently to the ground) with ten kilometers (about six miles) to go. Once back on his bike, he launched a desperate, adrenaline-surged breakaway to put forty seconds on Ullrich and the rest of the pack. This was enough cushion to ensure a record-tying fifth Tour victory.

"Lance is willing to lay everything on the line," Stapleton continues, "drive people hard, ask for extra support—just demand the best from everyone around him. Other athletes are uncomfortable doing this. They don't want to get into a situation where they asked for extra stuff and then failed. In Sydney [the 2000 Olympics], he had USA Cycling jumping through hoops, asking for all kinds of extra support. Then he got third. That night there was a big celebration for his cancer anniversary. With his family, friends, and supporters there, he got up and said, 'Hey, I did my best and I didn't get the gold. I know you expected better, you went the extra mile for me to come clear out here, and I lost and I'm sorry about that.' And then he just let it go."

Mellow Johnny

Indeed, when I fetched Lance at the San Francisco Airport some forty hours later after his flight from Sydney and asked how his trip was, he sounded like a guy who'd just returned from vacation rather than a vanquished athlete in a jet lag–dazed state of mourning. He talked about his helicopter sightseeing ride over the city and the hilarious Aussie-isms he had learned from the pilot. "I asked the pilot if he could find us some kangaroos from up there," relates Lance. "He goes, 'Mate, around here kangaroos are rarer than rocking horse shit!'" Lance's disposition after the most significant "failure" of his pro cycling career is an important study in how to balance a killer competitive instinct with a relaxed carpe-diem approach to life. No wonder he loved the nickname I coined for him and debuted with a limo-driver sign at the airport that day: Mellow Johnny (my "dumb American" pronunciation of *maillot jaune*, the French term for "yellow jersey"; the nickname was inspired by Stapleton's use of MJ as e-mail shorthand for Lance since he first donned the garment in 1999).

"Lance doesn't want to lose mainly because he doesn't want to let people down," Stapleton explains. "For him, the thought of showing up at the dinner table with the guys at the Tour and coming in second is horrifying [Lance called it the "walk of shame" on his Sirius satellite radio show in 2006]. He may be extremely driven by the downside of losing, but he's not afraid. During the Tour, I've seen Lance confirming arrangements for two hundred people from the Lance Armstrong Foundation to come to the Champs-Élysées to celebrate at the finish. I'm like, 'Uh, isn't that a little premature?' But he's not bothered by it; he doesn't give it a second thought," explains Stapleton.

"HE MAY BE EXTREMELY DRIVEN BY THE DOWNSIDE OF LOSING, BUT HE'S NOT AFRAID."

—Bill Stapleton

This thread leaves us with an extremely powerful albeit somewhat confusing moral: *Lance hates losing but is not afraid of it.* This fearless approach gave Lance the freedom to take the risks required to achieve peak performance and to continue to seek improvement even while at the top of the sport. This meant bringing new riders and new equipment to the team, risking the familiar for a potential improvement. It meant implementing new training techniques to address any perceived weaknesses and deeply analyzing even his smashing successes to discover areas for improvement. This powerful stance was a huge catalyst to help Lance go where no cyclist ever had—winning the Tour seven times in succession. Tiger Woods has also manifested this mind-set well, having twice broken down and rebuilt his golf swing (consequently struggling in competition until he could adapt to the swing changes) despite being the number one golfer in the world, simply because (as he told "60 Minutes"), "I'm always striving to get better . . . and in golf you never get there, you never arrive [at perfection]."

Many driven competitors who truly hate losing are also afraid of it. A potential competitive advantage is diminished by this latent fear, which leads to pressure, tension, and anxiety that compromise peak performance. Approaching a competitive challenge with a fearful, conservative mind-set is the perfect recipe for choking, something confirmed by the great cases of choking in sports history. This concept of not fearing defeat is often misinterpreted to mean, "Don't care about your performance." It's OK to fight hard to win, to want very badly to win, to strive for superficial rewards like money and recognition, but you must not determine your happiness or self-worth by the result. Stapleton reminds us that "in Lance's case, there is not a lot of failure to analyze. Nevertheless, when it happens he is able to let it go and move on. He eliminates failure and negative memories from his mind extremely well."

APPROACHING A COMPETITIVE CHALLENGE WITH A FEARFUL, CONSERVATIVE MIND-SET IS THE PERFECT RECIPE FOR CHOKING.

The Zen of Sweat

Pure confidence is a belief in one's ability to perform that transcends external variables and is validated only in the relevant competitive arena. As Lance says in *Every Second Counts*, "The world is full of people who are trying to purchase self-confidence, or manufacture it, or who simply posture it. But you can't fake confidence, you have to earn it. If you ask me, the only way to do that is work. You have to do the work."

Due to the prevailing myth that confidence is for sale through audiotapes, mental drills, or positive affirmations, many performers may believe they are confident, only to be fooled when called upon to perform under pressure. In this case, they possess confidence that is *situational*—vulnerable to outside variables. People with situational confidence are *reactive* under pressure. They anxiously alter their routine or strategy if an opponent presents an unexpected challenge. Someone in the workplace may get their bubble burst by a harsh comment from the boss during a presentation. Even the buoyant feeling of anticipation over a planned night out on the town can be killed by a flippant comment like, "You look kinda fat in that outfit." The net effect in each case is falling prey to negative thoughts and emotions that hamper your performance and enjoyment of life.

I asked Lance if he utilized anything beyond hard work—such as mental training or focusing techniques—to hone his confidence. "Nah, I'm not a real Zen-type person, at least I don't think that I am. I'm more of a mechanical-type person. I like to get into the rhythm of physically training hard, seeing the courses—hands-on physical work. Once I do that, everything else comes together. If I prepare my body properly and know what to expect with the racecourse—mentally, that is the best preparation for me. Superstitions, rituals, sitting in a dark room focused on every curve and every hill—I have no use for this type of preparation. For me, knowing that I've done all the work is a magical feeling," explains Lance. "When I'm on the starting line knowing that I've worked harder than anyone else—that is a great source of strength and inspiration for me."

Much has been made of Lance's work ethic and attention to detail in preparing for the Tour de France. Physically, he was devoted to a year-round scientifically designed heart rate–based training schedule. He conducted frequent fitness assessments gauging his ability to produce watts of power versus lactate accumulation in the bloodstream. Strategically, he and his advisers left no stone unturned when it came to selecting the proper team, staff, and equipment; conducting reconnaissance training camps to learn every nuance of the race routes; and ensuring that everyone in the organization was devoted to the singular cause of getting Lance into the yellow jersey.

> "WHEN I'M ON THE STARTING LINE KNOWING THAT I'VE WORKED HARDER THAN ANYONE ELSE— THAT IS A GREAT SOURCE OF STRENGTH AND INSPIRATION FOR ME."
>
> —Lance Armstrong

When Lance says, "You have to do the work," he means you have to do the *right* work. Many misinterpret the concept of "hard work," believing that merely putting in hours is the ticket to success—like the college student who highlighted every sentence in the textbook. Lance's oft-stated postcancer goal with his cycling career was to "do the sport correctly." This is a brilliant, but rarely expressed, sentiment for an athlete. Athletes more commonly speak in terms of training harder, putting in more mileage, and getting tougher, more focused, or more committed. To be sure, "more" is often a key component to evolve performance level, but often the answers for peak performance lie in the subtleties of one's approach. Indiscriminate hard work by an endurance athlete will lead to overtraining, while resting with an increased devotion away from training can result in dramatic breakthroughs. The salesperson focused on volume, numbers, and dogged determination will often find herself leaving voice mails for a potential customer, while that person is out playing golf and having sushi with a suitor who was creative enough to make a personal connection with, instead of a rote solicitation of, a prospect.

Boom Boom Bop

With confidence, you've either got it or you don't. And if you don't have it, even a skilled performer can be pulled off center and be negatively influenced by external variables. Playing on Centre Court at Wimbledon in front of fifteen thousand is different from playing on an outer court with an audience of four hundred. It's next to impossible to describe just how it is different inside the mind and body of the athlete—what exactly happens under pressure that enables those endowed with the X Factor to thrive and causes others to cave in.

> LANCE'S OFT-STATED POSTCANCER GOAL WITH HIS CYCLING CAREER WAS TO "DO THE SPORT CORRECTLY."

We know all about the dynamics of frail mentality, choking, and getting psyched out. We can relate because we've all been there. Johnny G, creator of the Spinning indoor cycling program and accomplished ultramarathon cyclist, liked to say, "The psych ends when the pain begins." You can get psyched up all you want, spend time in dark rooms drinking magic potions and chanting success mantras, but when the gun goes off and the pain starts, all the psych-up in the world can evaporate into the naked reality of the competitive arena.

COCKY OR CONFIDENT?

Early in his career, many characterized Lance's attitude as cocky or immature. Champion athletes are trained to go for the kill, yet we expect ice cream and apple pie talk out of the other side of their mouths. With this distorted perspective, you can criticize an athlete for being cocky or brash instead of understanding an honest expression of pure confidence. Rip Esselstyn remembers an occasion that revealed Lance's improbable confidence and competitive spirit as a teenager. "It was the 1987 Bermuda International Triathlon," Esselstyn explains. "This was the richest race in the sport with all the big stars present, nationally televised on NBC. After leading the swim and the early stages of the bike, Lance was caught from behind by the duo of Mike Pigg and Mark Allen, the top two triathletes in the world. Instead of deferentially dropping back, Lance gamely held on, matching their pace from close behind."

Esselstyn, who caught part of the scene on the road as a competitor and the rest on the NBC broadcast a few weeks later, recalls, "Pigg looked back, incredulous that he couldn't shake a teenager. He naturally suspected that Lance was gaining an unfair advantage by drafting." Following in the slipstream of a rider ahead was illegal in triathlon; rules mandated that you had to ride seven and a half meters behind the rider in front or be disqualified. Lance, closely watched by officials in the front of the pack, was no doubt observing the rule. However, one can still gain a slight, if continually diminishing, advantage by riding, say, eight, ten, or fifteen meters behind another rider. The mental advantage of keying off a pacemaker ahead is also significant.

Esselstyn continues, "Pigg turned around and screamed at Lance, 'Get the f— off my wheel!' To this Lance responded without hesitation, 'F—- you!' There were a lot of sound bleeps on that broadcast. You have Pigg and Allen, the top two guys in the history of the sport, on national TV, and young Lance won't give an inch—incredible!"

The football team at my high school in Los Angeles had the good fortune one year to host the number one ranked team in the nation in an early-season game. Much was made of this big showdown and our chance to knock off the baddest dudes in America. The school staged a pep rally with cute cheerleaders and players smashing through painted banners amid students on the campus quad screaming for an upset.

On the big night, our team burst onto the field screaming and yelling, buoyed by the frenetic energy of the home crowd. Warm-up exercises were crisp and focused, the captain's voice boomed with military authority—even the water boys were pumped up. I drifted over to the chain-link fence adjacent to the visitors' locker room and witnessed the visiting players calmly walking to the field in a single-file line. No screaming, no whooping, no running around in circles like zombies—just walking in a single-file line. The only sound was of rhythmic clapping—hands slapping the thighs twice, then clapping together once—boom boom bop, boom boom bop, boom boom bop.

As our team and crowd witnessed this procession of the finest high school football team in the nation coming to do some business in our house, the frenetic energy dissipated like a deflating balloon. The mere sight of these man-child football players, clad in ominous all-black uniforms and helmets, was enough to crush the collective spirit of our team and every supporter in the stadium before the opening kickoff. The final score was Banning 65, Taft 10—my school being the one named after the portly president.

We spend much time hoping, praying, rehearsing, and preparing in hopes that when showtime arrives, we have the confidence to perform under pressure. It may be, however, that we are looking for inspiration in the wrong places, endlessly tweaking our instruments to fly through the clouds instead of simply flying above them. Pure confidence cannot be gained this way. It can only be gained, as Lance says, by "doing the work."

The Four-Second Mile

Someone with pure confidence is *proactive* under pressure. Emotions and behavior are carefully controlled, while personal routine and competitive focus remain the same regardless of competitive standing or whether it's the Olympics or a casual competition. When an athlete or a team possesses pure confidence, they can rise to the occasion when it counts the most, sometimes performing at a level so extraordinary that it's beyond imagination. The greatest performances in sports history are far too implausible to set odds on. What we witness is the magical power of the human to transcend normal boundaries and limitations of energy, time, and space and perform on a supernatural plane: Reggie Jackson hitting three home runs with three swings in a 1978 World Series game, Tiger Woods winning the 2000 U.S. Open by fifteen strokes, and Lance Armstrong, body and spirit ravaged by cancer, coming back to win the most grueling athletic event in the world seven consecutive times.

It's awesome, unexplainable, and great fun to watch. I once read in a Taoist philosophy book about the concept of man transcending the space-time plane we believe we exist in to perform extraordinary feats. The author made the argument that athletic records could continue to be bettered infinitely. This phenomenon would manifest to the extent that the 100-meter dash contestants would vaporize and instantaneously cross the track at the speed of light. Forget about the four-minute mile, now it's the four-*second* mile! I wouldn't go that far, but there is a valid point.

Lance was able to transcend normal pain thresholds in the interest of climbing mountains quickly or riding his bike thirty-two miles in an hour time trial. He had a strong resolve to explore beyond the normal boundaries of human performance, to push harder instead of back off when the pain was at its worst. His mindset was impervious to fear, anxiety, or arbitrary limitations like the expectations of others, existing record times, or even the caliber of his competitors.

Pure Motivation = Pure Confidence

So how does one acquire this elusive pure confidence? For starters, you must commit to something bigger than winning and losing. As discussed in the chapter on clarity of purpose, the most powerful source of motivation is not victory in competition, financial gain, or some other external recognition but rather the pure love of the experience.

For the high school football team, a better choice than striving for an impossible upset of a vastly superior team would have been to play their hardest against the other team. In doing so, they would have achieved a growth experience, regardless of the final score. With a pure motivation you receive gratification internally rather than from the fickle outside world. Even if you stink at something, you can still have great fun, because it's possible to improve—to excel by your self-defined standards. If this book were to be torched by critics and sell only fifty-seven copies, I would naturally be disappointed. However, that eventuality would do nothing to minimize my greatest rewards. These came from the excitement, inspiration, and challenges I experienced during the journey of writing the book.

If you can wade through the macho hype and bravado that characterize modern sports, you will understand the nature of Lance's confidence as something different from what appears at first glance. Was Lance confident that he would win the Tour? Well, not so much as he was confident that he had prepared properly and could deliver his best effort. He knew on the starting line that he had worked harder and prepared better than anyone else and was willing to do whatever it took to win. He wanted to win very badly, but he was never certain or overconfident about winning. This type of mind-set has been the kiss of death for many performers and teams in sports, business, school, and elsewhere.

THE PERSON WHO OBSESSES ON A MEASURABLE END RESULT . . . WILL STRUGGLE WITH CONFIDENCE MORE THAN SOMEONE WHO IS COMMITTED TO THE PROCESS AND NOT ATTACHED TO THE OUTCOME.

As one who chooses his words very carefully, Lance was skilled at reminding us where he was coming from—if we paid close attention. When he enjoyed a defining stage win in the middle of the 2000 Tour, victory seemed assured. Yet when asked if he wanted champagne served at the team dinner that evening, he balked. "If we win in Paris, there will be champagne." While the winner may be virtually assured by the third quarter of a football blowout, victory was never assured for Lance until he crossed the finish line in Paris. Were he to crash on his bicycle a mile from the line and be unable to continue, his Tour would be lost—even though it was 99.99 percent complete.

The distinction in Lance's mind-set between confidence in his preparation and abilities and being confident of victory is critical, because it is the difference between pure confidence and situational confidence. The person who obsesses on a measurable end result, such as getting straight As, losing ten pounds, or winning sales agent of the quarter, will struggle with confidence more than someone who is committed to the process and not attached to the outcome. Only then can you truly experience the phenomenon of pure confidence and be unencumbered by the monster that contributes more to choking than anything else: fear of failure.

Honor the Jersey

In 1999, 2000, 2001, 2002, 2004, and 2005, Lance punctuated his Tour de France victories by winning the final time trial competition. (In 2003 he was third, fourteen seconds behind the winner—the previously mentioned stage where he chose to ride conservatively and avoid a crash like the one that befell Ullrich on the slippery, rainy course.) While winning time trials is an expected ingredient in winning the yellow jersey, there is something below the surface quite profound about these final time trial results: Lance had a virtually insurmountable lead before the stage every time! His stated motivation, "I always feel it's important for the *maillot jaune* to race the final time trial with 100 percent effort and prove that he's the best rider in the race and that he deserves to win the Tour de France," is flimsy in comparison to the risk of riding aggressively and risking a potential Tour-losing crash.

Lance hammering the final time trial (typically contested the day before the final, mostly ceremonial, stage into Paris) goes way beyond honoring the yellow jersey; it's the essence of his legacy as an athlete and a motivational icon. Imagine Lance—sitting pretty with a certain overall victory and many more millions of dollars (his Tour victory bonus was $5 million in 2004 and escalated to $10 million in 2005)—setting forth to engulf his legs and lungs in pain for an hour and risking everything each time he turned a corner for a payoff of essentially nothing. Why? Nearly anyone else in that position would cash in their chips and go home ahead—ride along conservatively, take an acceptable twelfth place, and preserve the yellow jersey. Lance, on the other hand, couldn't help himself. His motivation was so pure that his consciousness transcended winning and losing such that he became completely absorbed in the moment and living life to the fullest: carpe diem, as he likes to say.

Protecting a lead and what's rightfully yours is shrewd and honorable by all measures. But if you were to occasionally tiptoe up to the edge of the cliff, take a deep breath, and leap into the unknown beyond your comfort zone and perceived limitations, you may achieve a huge growth experience. Sure, the scale of your dreams and corresponding risks may be set in a sensible manner. It's not cool to second-mortgage your home to load up on a penny stock or paddle out into sixteen-foot surf on Oahu's North Shore if your home venue is the Breakers Water Park ("a tidal wave of fun") in Tucson. Judging from the epidemic of self-limiting beliefs, negativity, and fear in society, however, many of us would be well served to take a few more leaps out of our patterned, regulated, and conventional lives.

Have you recently—or ever—pushed your body to the limit? You know, run as fast as you can for a certain distance or keep doing reps until your muscles completely fail—then rest two minutes and do it again? What about challenging your mind? Do you have a commitment to acquire new knowledge and skills, or are you cruising along, content to get through the day and spew forth self-limiting statements and beliefs when necessary? ("Sorry, I'm terrible with names—what's yours again?" "Oh, you're a triathlete? Me too: drink beer, punch the remote control, and get up for another beer, ha ha ha!" "Watch this shot—I have no idea where it's going; haven't played in months.") Yes, it's a free society, and you have every right to punch the code on your electric gate, roll into the garage, zap some packaged food, settle in, and enjoy your TiVo or Netflix on a high-definition screen with surround sound. However, there is indisputable value in pushing your boundaries and assimilating the consequent lessons of success or failure. When you live a high-definition life, you become better, stronger, and happier.

WHEN YOU LIVE A HIGH-DEFINITION LIFE, YOU BECOME BETTER, STRONGER, AND HAPPIER.

Accounting for Your Clear Purpose

It's a challenge to cultivate pure confidence in the modern world, because there are massive forces trying to break your will and shatter your confidence. Before the 2006 Winter Olympics, American downhill skier Bode Miller mentioned that he might skip the Games because he was turned off by the hype. This comment generated plenty of shock value, considering that Bode was *the* headline/multiple magazine cover athlete leading up to the Games.

In his refreshingly raw and often politically incorrect tone, Bode contrasted the Olympic Creed with the media-driven, overdramatized, medal count–obsessed show that the modern Olympics have become. The Olympic Creed, from Baron Pierre de Coubertin (founder of the modern Games), reads:

The important thing in the Olympic Games is not to win but to take part, just as the important thing in life is not the triumph but the struggle.

"Now does that sound like the Olympics to you?" Bode asked in a 2006 *Newsweek* magazine interview. "The Olympics are about getting that gold medal or you're a loser. The Olympics are just not a pure thing anymore."

You may not agree with Bode, and you may even be disgusted by his attitude, captured by his post-Olympic comment that he was satisfied with his Olympic experience (despite being shut out of the medals in his five events) because he "got to party and socialize at an Olympic level." Many, including Lance, thought that Bode owed it to America to take the Games more seriously. (Bode was heavily criticized for his "Doping should be legalized" rant in a January 2006 *Rolling Stone* magazine article in which he grouped Lance with Barry Bonds, informing us that "Those guys are knowingly cheating.") Bode acts like he owes nobody nothin' (a problematic stance for an athlete at his level, getting paid the beaucoup bucks by sponsors to win), but he may be approaching his athletic goals with a mind-set ideally suited to his personality. He's no Lance Armstrong, but he and his "party on, dude" approach won him the 2004 World Cup and the title of the top overall skier in the world.

Making the Grade

From the time we start elementary school, we are programmed to measure and judge ourselves and others on a superficial, material level. In California, public education has become so obsessed with standardized test score performance that subjects like physical education, art, music, and other "superfluous" educational pursuits have been mercilessly cut from the curriculum to save money. It seems as though we want to develop unfit, one-dimensional adults to push papers and punch keyboards in an office. The creative child who may not thrive in a regimented educational environment will have difficulty developing pure confidence, let alone the other success factors, when handcuffed by the system we have in place.

Teenagers I speak to feel a tremendous cultural pressure to pursue the fast track to success, which they have been brainwashed to believe is getting good grades to gain entry into a top college, which leads to a high-paying job, which leads to the American dream of making and spending money. With that to look forward to, no wonder high school is such a difficult time for these kids.

Falling prey to this rat-race mentality suppresses our free spirit, stunts personal growth, and can cause great talent to slip through the cracks. If you buy into the superficial definition of *beauty*, how can you become totally confident in your appearance? If you buy into the materialistic definition of success, how can you develop the confidence to depart from the beaten path to pursue your passion if guaranteed income is one of your sacrifices?

So how do you become bulletproofed to cultural competitive pressures with an unshakable, unconditional confidence in your abilities? Positive attitude, clarity of purpose, and specialized intelligence are critical and thus precede this chapter. We often get led astray from the path of self-actualization because of our regimented systems and other harmful outside influences. I myself chose to minor in accounting in college, not because I had a passion for it but because a roommate informed me, "Dude! The big firms come onto campus to interview you. If you have decent grades, you get hired—just like that. For *twenty grand* a year!" (That was big chow in 1985.) Wow, a blissful future was assured—all I had to do was suffer through a set of boring accounting classes. No offense to the people who have a passion for the field; I'm merely illustrating how

I became diverted from my basic nature of a creative, self-directed free spirit to pursue the epitome of a corporate, detail-oriented, tightly structured, and constrained career. In light of the fact that "creative accountants" often go to jail, creative writing might have been a better fit. There is nothing wrong with the ambition to enter the workforce and pursue a career direction. I think we would all be better served, however, to encourage a more aggressive and unrestrained exploration of the options for career and life direction—among our youth and among ourselves. It's never too late to make a career change, and it's never too early to expand your thinking beyond the normal channels of the rat race.

ONE HOME RUN

Like Lance on the bike, many great success stories in the business world have a common theme of clear purpose, undying confidence, and positive attitude—even in the face of struggle and failure. Mark Sisson, a former 2:18 marathoner and fourth-place finisher in the 1982 Hawaii Ironman, has had a circuitous entrepreneurial journey that today finds him owning and operating a successful nutritional supplement business, Primal Nutrition, in Malibu, California.

In college Sisson was a premed student who occupied his spare time remodeling his dorm room. Bolstered by accolades on his design and building skills, he put med school on hold and decided to build and paint houses while he pursued a competitive running and triathlon career after graduation. Satiated after his Ironman performance, he then drifted into the business world, operating a frozen yogurt shop and later a restaurant. After dabbling in acting, broadcasting, and personal training and serving as chief executive of USA Triathlon (the national governing body of the sport), Sisson climbed up the ladder at a large vitamin supplement company to the post of chief operating officer.

At the age of forty-three, with a family to support and no savings or equity, he departed the well-paying position to strike out on his own. "Although it was a wonderful career, I felt constrained by having a ceiling on my income, potential, and creative energy," he reflects. "My entrepreneurial spirit requires that I have no ceiling above me!" Building his own business from scratch was admittedly stressful, but not as stressful to Sisson as the constraints of corporate life. "My purpose was crystal clear at all times. This made me feel empowered and confident—even when I was stressed about the reality of going to bed each night with four mouths to feed," explains Sisson. "Whenever I run up against a problem, I remind myself that if it was easy, everyone would be doing it."

Five years after starting Primal Nutrition, Sisson became essentially set for life financially. He says that his convoluted path to success was irrelevant, for in business, "as long as you can survive year to year, you only have to hit one home run to win. Here in Los Angeles, there are tons of stories of actors and writers who lived hand to mouth for years and then hit it big. Without a clear purpose to keep them on track, those now-successful artists would have long since abandoned their craft." It's an inspiring way to look at the challenges of succeeding as an entrepreneur, where failure comes with the territory. Those who are able to assimilate failure—or simply a lack of "success"—into something positive and empowering are the ones who eventually hit the home run.

Reframing the Past

Another critical element in developing pure confidence is how you interpret past experiences, for these are the raw material for how your brain is wired today. The pure confidence I describe here is more than an intellectual concept; it is truly a state of being. As discussed in the chapter on positive attitude, stimulus from the outside world elicits an emotional, chemical reaction in our bodies. Based upon our interpretation of the stimulus, the hypothalamus directs certain chemicals to flood the bloodstream, affecting the brain and other areas of the body.

THOSE WHO ARE ABLE TO ASSIMILATE FAILURE— OR SIMPLY A LACK OF "SUCCESS"—INTO SOMETHING POSITIVE AND EMPOWERING ARE THE ONES WHO EVENTUALLY HIT THE HOME RUN.

There are many familiar examples of this phenomenon that confirm its scientific truth for us. When you step on the starting line of a race, stand in front of a large group to deliver a speech, or ask a girl to dance at the junior high sock hop, your chemical and emotional state is altered in a powerful manner. For many faced with stressful events, negative emotions like fear and anxiety define our state of being and hamper peak performance. Even worse, the neurons in the brain learn from these experiences and hardwire themselves such that the identical chemical experience will occur over and over.

As you might imagine, it becomes extremely difficult to rewire the brain to overcome these core personality components. This is confirmed by the futility of psyching up for a fearful event. You can think positive, empowering thoughts for months on end leading up

IT'S NEVER TOO LATE TO MAKE A CAREER CHANGE, AND IT'S NEVER TOO EARLY TO EXPAND YOUR THINKING BEYOND THE NORMAL CHANNELS OF THE RAT RACE.

to the big speech, dance, or race, but all that empowerment will disappear when the event is upon you and your body is overwhelmed by a trained chemical response. The power of psycho-altering drugs like alcohol, prescription antidepressants, and illegal substances to override the body's natural response is no doubt a large factor in their popularity.

The natural way to develop pure confidence involves rewiring your brain so that you are able to effortlessly enter the zone, as described in Chapter 2. This requires more than just intellectually understanding a concept in a book. You must rise to the challenge of interpreting the past, present, and future differently. The starting point would be to raise your awareness of what is going on in your body when you are faced with a powerful external stimulus that alters your body chemistry and your emotions.

Lance often says that if he had to choose between suffering from cancer and winning the Tour de France, he would choose the cancer because it changed his life—and the lives of the millions he has inspired—in a powerful and positive way. Discussing the memory of his cancer experience in *Every Second Counts*, he says, "You can alter any experience in your mind . . . it takes practice, but it's possible." He then explains how he put a positive spin on even the depths of his suffering—imagining that his chemo-induced vomiting represented the cancer leaving his body.

Most people lead an extremely programmed life where they are disconnected from their emotions and a higher self-awareness of what governs their behavior patterns. Leading new-age thinker Dr. Deepak Chopra, who wrote *Ageless Body, Timeless Mind*, has an interesting characterization for the ultimate level of consciousness. At a lecture I attended, Chopra urged us, the audience, to consider ourselves a "swirling mass of atoms, expressing their potential as a human form known as [Brad Kearns]." This is a true statement in the quantum physical sense. With this thinking, there is no separation between mind and body or even the rest of the matter in the universe, which makes us merely "silent observers" of what is happening around us.

"YOU CAN ALTER ANY EXPERIENCE IN YOUR MIND . . . IT TAKES PRACTICE, BUT IT'S POSSIBLE."

—Lance Armstrong

Thinking in this paradigm opens us up to greater possibilities, as it means we can perceive the world any way we want to. For example, the saying "Time flies when you're having fun" is true in a literal sense. Lifting a simplified insight from Einstein's theory of relativity and other scientific work, we can understand how the passage of time is dependent upon the perception of the observer. Sure, we have clocks that can measure sixty seconds per minute and sixty minutes per hour, but these concrete measurements mean nothing without someone interpreting them into reference points. Consider if you were to go on an hour-long bike ride with Lance while he was in peak form training for the Tour de France. It would surely be sixty minutes for both you and he, but it would likely have a different meaning to your mind and body. Lance would likely bid you adieu and then carry on for a few more hours at a faster pace, while you may find yourself dialing the mobile ambulance rescue line for a lift to the nearest ER.

Chopra's central premise in *Ageless Body, Timeless Mind* is that we can overcome the aging paradigm merely by believing something different from the accepted premise that we are born as separate beings, grow old, and then die. If we believe ourselves to be a swirling mass of atoms, one with the universe, with our atoms renewing at an amazing rate (literally speaking, we manufacture a new stomach lining every five days and a new liver every six weeks, and 98 percent of the atoms in our body have been exchanged for new ones each year), we can discard the aging paradigm, extend life span, and improve well-being dramatically. Chopra cites extensive scientific studies that identify "youthful spirit" as perhaps the most profound longevity factor among centenarians around the globe.

Why this detour to new-age land? It's relevant if you wish to rewire your brain chemistry to face your challenges with more confidence. Look back at your time in high school and consider how you felt about your grades and SAT scores, competitive athletics, or the tribulations of your romantic relationships. Today these issues are virtually meaningless to your daily life and no longer elicit the same powerful emotional response that occurred when you were experiencing them. Hence, it is possible for any of us to manipulate our interpretation of the challenges we face every day.

If you have a peak performance goal in the fitness/athletic arena or in your business career or you wish to simply lead a balanced life, yet find nerves or lack of confidence getting in the way, you must strive to interpret your past experience and your future outlook toward this goal in a different way. Memories of emotions that are negative must be destroyed and reframed into something positive. If you have struggled with weight-loss efforts and have a negative attitude about your diet, appearance, or exercise program, you must clean your slate and start over. Be thankful that you have a body that works the way it does, and understand that the body is incredibly good at adapting to how you treat it. If you alter your diet, exercise program, and lifestyle in the direction of health and fitness, it is a certainty (barring a serious medical condition) that your body will drop excess fat in response to the stimulus you place upon it. If you are having difficulty balancing your career aspirations and time commitment at work with spending quality time with family, perhaps you can gain perspective from others with experience in a similar situation or from the popular saying (sometimes attributed to the *Peanuts* character Charlie Brown) "Nobody ever went to their death bed wishing they had spent more time at the office."

STEPS TO DEVELOP SUCCESS FACTOR 4: PURE CONFIDENCE

1. **Play the game.** Pure confidence is developed only from intensive preparation and repeated exposure to high-pressure competitive situations. Lance did not win the Tour de France by sitting around contemplating winning the Tour de France. Do the work required to get yourself ready, and then get into the game! Internalize both success and failure in a positive and empowering manner, learning from experience so that you may improve in the future.

2. **Be proactive.** Stick to your game plan and refuse to be intimidated by opponents or discouraged by external variables that commonly throw off those with situational confidence. As Bill Stapleton reminds us, "Lance never panicked when things got difficult in the Tour. He was never anxious or scared." If you find

yourself feeling anxious before a peak performance effort, refocus on simply delivering your own best effort and stop worrying about things you can't control.

3. Appreciate the process. Pure confidence transcends external variables, even the end result of your pursuits. When you are motivated by the enjoyment of the process, you obtain your gratification internally and nurture your confidence by succeeding according to your own standards instead of those of the judgmental outside world. Instead of just following the beaten path, leverage the powerful link between clarity of purpose and pure confidence by pursuing goals that turn you on.

4. Reframe the past. Rewire your brain for success by raising your awareness of negative thought patterns and stored emotional memories of past experiences. Reframe memories or your perspective (such as Chopra's example with aging) into positive and empowering thoughts. Rid yourself of excess mental baggage, and approach present and future challenges with a clean slate.

Graham Watson, grahamwatson.com

8

KEEP YOUR
OWN SCORECARD

P eak performers come in all shapes and sizes and with widely varying approaches. Unfortunately, we have developed an insecurity-driven penchant to worship and blindly mirror the approach of the successful—something that does not work, as many coaches, mentors, and parents have discovered the hard way. Instead, as with the contrasting success approaches of Lance and Jan Ullrich, we should use our own intuitive powers to pull relevant insights from champions like Lance and thoughtfully apply them to our own lives in the manner that we best see fit. If you are a cerebral/analytical type, your experience of reading this book and applying the success factors may look completely different from the experience of someone who is a creative/emotional type.

Regardless of the mechanics of your approach and even the nature of your goals, you must create life circumstances that will propel you to achieve peak performance. The connection fans and media breezily make between Lance's cancer ordeal and his eventual success in the Tour de France (lost weight, became more focused, toughed out the pain, and so on) can cause one to gloss over the fact that his illness was nevertheless a devastating setback to his athletic career. It's just that Lance chose to turn this setback into a success, thanks to a positive attitude, clarity of purpose, specialized intelligence, and pure confidence.

Wherever you are today, you can do the same thing by understanding that the secret to success lies within you; the fruit is ripe and has fallen at your feet, so stop looking for answers on the high branches in someone else's yard. Inside you is the "greatest human freedom"—the ability to choose a positive attitude. Wherever you are today, you must be resolute to apply this asset against the ever-present opponent of bad air in the world. As Lance reminds us, the way you express your positive attitude is personal. You don't have to win the peppy, smiley school spirit award, and you don't have to have ideal circumstances or attributes. You just have to harness your mental ability to make the ultimate empowering choice.

Next you must pursue the highest expression of your talents, filtering out cultural pressures to be someone that you are not and embracing your unique gifts to obtain clarity of purpose. Yes, it's hard—but it's the only way to give yourself a fair chance. And by the way, if you have kids, embracing their unique gifts and supporting them as they discover their own path is the only way to *not* screw them up! "I think the way to raise children is to treat them with respect, like a friend or a peer, pass along your lessons, and then watch them get out of your life," says Lance.

Sure, there are certain principles that are mandatory for success. You should surely "encourage" your kids to finish high school. College is a great idea if they want a professional career, but in that realm they should be given the flexibility to choose the best college, major, and study habits for their unique interests. For all of us, the most important thing is to discover and be true to our basic nature and measure success internally as we proceed along the path that we have chosen. As Bart Knaggs says in discussing his career aspirations, "I like to keep my own scorecard."

You must develop the specialized intelligence to blend intuitive and practical skills, learn from mistakes, and constantly evolve your approach in response to competitive stimuli. You must develop the patience and restraint to stay focused on a rewarding long-term plan. You must keep goals in perspective—releasing your attachment to the outcome—so that you can enjoy a happy, healthy life instead of an unbalanced one full of empty successes.

> ## "I THINK THE WAY TO RAISE CHILDREN IS TO TREAT THEM WITH RESPECT, LIKE A FRIEND OR A PEER, PASS ALONG YOUR LESSONS, AND THEN WATCH THEM GET OUT OF YOUR LIFE."
>
> —Lance Armstrong

With the powerful elements of these success factors in action, you can acquire the pure confidence of a champion. Resolve to approach your goals with a positive, proactive stance, playing the game when the stakes are high instead of spewing excuses from the sidelines. Discard self-limiting beliefs and negative memories to rewire your brain for success. Finally, you must reject the measuring, judging world that leaves you vulnerable to situational confidence and instead appreciate the beauty and rewards in the process.

Consider Lance, who had many hands clapping for him and many monies paid to him for his competitive exploits—someone who could leverage massive external motivators. And while these motivators certainly mattered to him, Lance as an endurance athlete had to be self-motivated in a more profound way than anyone.

After all, motivation is defined as "an incentive for action," and in his career as a cyclist, Lance took more action and burned more energy than arguably anyone else on the planet.

Journey Through the Fractal

"All the time, people ask me, 'What about Lance? How does he do it?'" says Bart Knaggs. "I do not think he was the most physically gifted rider out there. I don't think he has the ideal body type—maybe for a triathlete, but not a cyclist. The complexity of the Tour de France means that the most critical skill set is a clear head, total focus, and an indomitable will. In Daniel Coyle's *New York Times* article [February 5, 2006, called "That Which Does Not Kill Me Makes Me Stranger," about Slovenian ultramarathon cyclist Jure Robic and his mental instability that occurs when he stretches himself to the limit], there was some interesting research cited about the body's ability to override symptoms of pain and fatigue."

A quick summary: performance limitations, long thought to be in the muscles themselves (push too hard and muscle tissue becomes exhausted), could actually be in the brain instead. The brain makes the body slow down when it senses fatigue as a protection mechanism. As Dr. Timothy Noakes, South African exercise physiology professor and author of the eight-hundred-page seminal work on running training and physiology—*Lore of Running*—said in the *New York Times* article, "In fatigue, it only *feels* like we're going to die. The actual physiological risks that fatigue represents are essentially trivial."

Knaggs continues, "When you are able to leverage the power of the brain, you can push yourself out onto a precipice that is beyond what we perceive to be the limitations of human performance. It's an inherent mental ability that humans have in order to survive, just like a jackrabbit on the plains running for its life from a predator. Unfortunately, the conventions of our comfortable modern world have led us to believe that we can settle for less than our potential. The saying goes that we use only 10 percent of our brains. We probably use an even smaller percentage of our physical capabilities, because we have not unlocked the potential in our brains. For our own selfish reasons, perhaps to deny our own weaknesses and shortcomings, we encourage setting limitations on people. We collectively do this in a very insidious manner. This kind of shit sells, because we accept standards that are not demanding.

"For example, I'm considered a good father by people in my peer group if I skip a golf game to watch my kids play soccer. In return, let's say Stapleton comes home early from a business trip; I'll tell him, 'You're a good dad.' *Are* we good dads? Offering and receiving compliments serve mutual purposes and we feel better about ourselves. We propagate that shit and support it because we are scared to face the brutal self-truth of how hard we actually work, how far we perform from our potential, the small percentage of our lives we are really taking advantage of. People don't want to deal with that. People want to be *placated*! They want to feel OK. They can't admit that they are lazy or untalented or barely scratching the level of what they can accomplish. We want to sleep in our air-conditioned homes, eat our little healthy snacks, and carry on just like everyone else.

"As humans, we like to assume that we know all the facts and are in control. When we are not, we like to turn to something bigger than ourselves, like religion, to feel in control. What really makes us think that something like space travel is impossible? Because it's beyond the realm of our experience. We think we understand the limits of human endurance and so forth. But I have news for you— there is one thing that can change it all: accessing the brain. When you access the potential of your brain, you can pursue the impossible. The brain takes you past the perceived limits of the body.

"On a basic level, a Tony Robbins tape can take you from your level-two [of your potential] rut to break through to level three.

Lance has discovered a way to access the potential in his brain and his body to break through from level seven to level eight. I believe that he has exercised longer and harder, with more intensity, than any other athlete in the history of the world. He discovered a fractal that allowed him to enter another dimension of human performance, where he could dance on this fuzzy line at the border of the unknown and seemingly intolerable suffering. And he actually delighted in it!" concludes Knaggs.

> "WHEN YOU ACCESS THE POTENTIAL OF YOUR BRAIN, YOU CAN PURSUE THE IMPOSSIBLE. THE BRAIN TAKES YOU PAST THE PERCEIVED LIMITS OF THE BODY."
>
> —Bart Knaggs

Army Clothes

You may not be inclined to explore the fuzzy line of royal suffering on a bicycle, but you can gain inspiration from this example to unlock greater potential for your own mind or body. For example, you may wonder where Lance got the energy to train harder than any other human and live a "go, go, go" lifestyle around the clock. Wouldn't it be great to have more energy in your daily life? Well, if you can view energy as a renewable resource instead of a fixed asset, you open yourself up to greater possibilities. Beyond regenerating your energy daily with sleep, a positive attitude and stimulating surroundings can increase your energy. After scoring forty-eight points and playing fifty-one minutes of a 2001 NBA championship series overtime game against the Lakers, Philadelphia 76ers star Allen Iverson was asked if fatigue was going to be a factor in the series: "I've been waiting for this opportunity all my life. I'm not thinking about fatigue right now. Fatigue is army clothes."

BEYOND REGENERATING YOUR ENERGY DAILY WITH SLEEP, A POSITIVE ATTITUDE AND STIMULATING SURROUNDINGS CAN INCREASE YOUR ENERGY.

We've all experienced the phenomenon of being tired at the end of a long day and not being up for a scheduled social gathering. You drag your feet with a negative attitude right up to the door, then enter and quickly experience a huge lift in your disposition and energy level. Your increase in energy here is a literal, scientific truth, like when you apply Deepak Chopra's "youthful spirit" concept to alter the aging paradigm. When you can boost your energy by eliminating bad air, bad vibes, and negative attitudes from your daily life (replacing them with good attitudes, good foods, good people, good movies, and so on), this is a wonderful example of accessing the power of the brain to extend your physical potential.

Consider the energy cost of going against Don Miguel Ruiz's admonition and taking things personally or playing emotionally manipulative games as a normal and customary course of business or daily life. As we learned from Bill Stapleton's and others' accounts of how Lance and his team dealt with the monumental pressures of high-stakes athletics intertwined with celebrity and cultural icon status, "honest, correct, and real" is standard operating procedure. Visualize Lance riding up the Alpe d'Huez engulfed by screaming, spitting mobs, and apply that metaphor to daily life. Jot down these blips on the back of a business card, and see if they can't improve your business:

- "When it's raining, I just put on a rain jacket and go."
- "In a life-or-death situation like my illness, I had no choice but to be positive."
- "I do lose sleep over [criticism] at times because I care. But you have to prioritize these things—think less about the bad stuff."
- "I never heard Lance complain about anything. [He] would never dwell on his defeats; he would always be thinking ahead to the next race."
- "Quit bitching."

Unfortunately, our brains are often filled with less empowering thoughts: "I'm too busy." "I wish things were different." "It's your fault." "I can't believe this happened to me, what bad luck!" "That's just not fair." Lance will face unfamiliar challenges in his postcycling life and must discover new ways to get the most out of his brain and body. The next time you are running around with kids and beg out because you are tired, you can inquire to that same authority that Lance consulted on his way up the mountains in the Tour. "Am I really fatigued? Am I a good parent? Am I enjoying my life and expressing my talents fully? Or am I measuring myself externally against the conventions of the modern world in hopes of feeling placated?"

Whether you have been fortunate enough to achieve great things or are immersed in a challenge and yet to achieve your goals, you can sit back and expand your perspective about this game of life that we play. You can focus not only on the accomplishment but on getting there with integrity and class (like Lance waiting for a fallen opponent to resume a fair race), thereby serving as an inspiration and a role model for others. Then you can appreciate everyday life as a continual opportunity to better yourself at every corner, access more of your brain, and break through self-limiting beliefs and behavior patterns.

PERHAPS YOU HAVE EVERYTHING YOU *NEED* RIGHT NOW AND CAN EVOLVE TO FOCUS ON WHAT YOU *DESERVE* IN YOUR LIFE.

Adopting this disposition is not simple. As author and Pulitzer Prize–winning columnist Anna Quindlen says, "The truth about your own life is not always easy to accept and sometimes hasn't even occurred to you." If we are motivated to seek pleasure or avoid pain, sometimes we can deftly avoid pain by not trying or not dealing with our issues. Witness the schoolchild who asks to sit out from the running competition so as not to endure any disappointment or ridicule or the adult who crafts a compelling, convoluted sob story for his predicament of being in a level-two rut. Consequently, the "seek pleasure" endeavors, like improving skills, increasing energy, and achieving goals, can often drop to the bottom of the to-do list. Instead, dreams are squelched by complaining and rationalizing, and we fill our days with the endless distractions offered by technology, consumerism, and fanaticism.

If you can internalize the moral of Lance's success factors and recalibrate your approach accordingly, you can win small victories every day. Start an exercise program, quit smoking, or leave work at 5 P.M. every day because it makes you feel better instead of because you feel like you need to. Perhaps you have everything you *need* right now and can evolve to focus on what you *deserve* in your life. Then, instead of being motivated by guilt and cultural pressure to measure up to some artificial standard, you will be motivated by the pure joy of exploration and accomplishment that is fundamental to our human nature.

Curing Cancer and Other Retirement Hobbies

Bart Knaggs comments, "I have a great degree of admiration for Lance's accomplishments. Intellectually, they provide evidence in my belief in the power of the brain to bring the body to a higher level. Being close to Lance, it causes me to reflect on my own potential. Just as I've discussed about Lance's success factors, I can turn that around on myself and ask, 'What are you doing, guy? Are you doing all that you can do?' I help Lance win races, get endorsement deals, invest in real estate and hedge funds, and so on, but do I want to be important independently of Lance, in my own way?

"I've come to the conclusion that I am an expert at riding shotgun. When Lance got sick, I got involved, researched everything I possibly could about the disease, and helped Lance become an advocate for his treatment. With the Discovery team, I'll oversee the technology research and development projects to enable Lance, the team, and sponsors to realize the vision of gaining a competitive advantage and remaining on the cutting edge. With Stapleton, I might come up with a big-picture vision of how we can help a sponsor tap into a market where they are losing traction, and with my insight, I'll empower Stapleton to do what he does best—pitch the concept to the sponsor and close the deal.

"Lance was meant to do great things with his life, and there are not many truly exceptional people like that. Now that he is retired from cycling, I believe Lance has the potential to do something even greater for the cancer community. People think he is doing great things now, what with the Lance Armstrong Foundation raising $114 million and increasing awareness with sixty million [both as of mid-2006] yellow bands. But I don't think we are going deep enough. We listen to scientists say that a cure is impossible or fifty years away. So we settle for a goal like making cancer patients more comfortable." Knaggs, who lost his younger brother David to leukemia in 2003, continues, "This kind of attitude bugs the shit out of me, because we are selling ourselves short.

"If we can turn the example of Lance's performing the impossible on the bike to a new challenge, we can pursue a cure for cancer. With cancer, we are like Lance the cyclist back in 1995—the winner of the prestigious Liege-Bastogne-Liege bike race in Europe. But with our present perspective, who the hell cares about Liege-Bastogne-Liege? No one realized he was performing below his potential. If we apply the analogy of winning the Tour de France to cancer, we should set our sights on curing cancer. If I can have a small part in that, helping to guide, direct, and shape Lance to fulfill his potential in that direction, then I will be honoring the example of Lance and contributing to something bigger than myself and my own personal needs," concludes Knaggs.

By all accounts Lance is up for the challenge, choosing to direct tremendous time and energy toward raising awareness of and lobbying the government for additional funding for cancer research, always with his trademark directness and competitive intensity. "My mission now is bigger than winning the Tour de France," he said in a June 2006 *USA Today* interview. At an appearance on "The Charlie Rose Show" that month, he told his host, "Now is not the time to cut funding at the National Cancer Institute, which they have done for the first time in the last thirty-five years. I asked the president [at an August 2005 visit to Bush's ranch in Crawford, Texas, where they shared a much-publicized mountain-bike ride] for a billion dollars. He said, 'I'll get back to you on that,'" Lance laughed. "I'm still working on it. I reminded him and everybody in the administration and both sides [political parties] that we're not going away, we are going to be here and continue to raise the issue and encourage other people to raise the issue."

Lance has received accolades on Capitol Hill from the likes of Senator Tom Harkin (D-Iowa), who told *USA Today*, "Not only is he a national hero, he's a world-class advocate for cancer research. His example resonates with cancer patients. He has great access to senators and congressmen, and he really knows what he's talking about."

Building Your Foundation

This book is about achieving peak performance, taking inspiration from the ultimate peak performer, Lance Armstrong. Sometimes, however, you aren't ready for or interested in peak performance. The stresses, pressures, and setbacks of daily life steal your energy and lead to discouragement, depression, and exhaustion. So what's the secret to preventing, fighting, or overcoming this? Give up. Give in. Go with the flow and accept that failure and disappointment are a natural, necessary, and enriching part of life.

The movie *The Weather Man* followed Nicolas Cage's title character as he rose to the top of his profession but was burdened by a feeling of insignificance ("I receive a large reward for pretty much zero effort and contribution") and a shattered family life. At the end of the film, Cage's character delivers a voice-over monologue while the camera shows him walking down a crowded sidewalk. As he talks, special effects steadily evaporate the number of people around him, until he is finally walking alone. "I remember once imagining what my life would be like, what I'd be like," Cage's character says. "I pictured having all these qualities. Strong, positive qualities that people could pick up on from across a room. But as time passed, few ever became qualities I actually had. And all the possibilities I faced, and the sorts of people I could be—all of them got reduced every year to fewer and fewer. Until finally they got reduced to one—to who I am. And that's who I am. . . . Things didn't work out the way I predicted. Accepting that's not easy. But easy doesn't enter into grown-up life."

Everyone has this same truth. Yep, even Lance Armstrong. It is important to accept that you may not realize all of your dreams and that bad stuff can happen to you. You have to deal with it and then carry on with grace and a positive attitude. If you cannot be at peace with the reality of your life, you may wake up one day and find yourself living a lie—a lie covered up expertly by the accumulation of material "things" or by insincere behavior instead of honesty. It's like winning a race but no one claps because you have no friends or like making a million bucks a year delivering the weather on a national morning show in New York while "some other guy is living with my family in Chicago."

> IF YOU CANNOT BE AT PEACE WITH THE REALITY OF YOUR LIFE, YOU MAY WAKE UP ONE DAY AND FIND YOURSELF LIVING A LIE.

Vulnerability = Power

At a seminar I attended a few years ago, the facilitator wrote a message on the board that said, "Vulnerability = Power." I didn't understand it at first. Being the competitive athlete that I was, I had always envisioned power as force, domination, intimidation—taking a pseudo-casual sip from the water bottle as you fly by a struggling competitor on a steep hill. But if you define power as the ability to motivate, inspire, and change your life and the lives of others around you, then nothing is more powerful than being vulnerable.

> IF YOU DEFINE POWER AS THE ABILITY TO MOTIVATE, INSPIRE, AND CHANGE YOUR LIFE AND THE LIVES OF OTHERS AROUND YOU, THEN NOTHING IS MORE POWERFUL THAN BEING VULNERABLE.

This is the critical but often misunderstood connection (that Lance has taken great pains to explain to willing listeners) between Lance struggling for his life in a hospital bed and winning the Tour de France. Cancer made Lance—the young, rich, unbreakable guy with the World title and the Porsche and the hella-rad new house on the lake—vulnerable for the first time. When he humbly submitted to something larger than himself—his cancer ordeal—he discovered the key to unlock his extraordinary potential as an athlete and, more important, as a person.

Did you know that Lance, Bart Knaggs, and a few others spearheaded the creation of the Lance Armstrong Foundation in the fall of 1996—*while* Lance was undergoing chemotherapy treatment?! He had a compelling desire to give back at his most vulnerable time, when he had nothing to give and was fighting for his own life. This is a far more profound sign of a champion than the mounted and framed yellow jerseys on his wall. This would be a good thing to reflect upon for a moment, particularly if you feel a tiny inclination to dismiss Lance's commentary about being motivated by love of the sport, instead of by money and fame, as politically correct jock-speak. Or if you are quick to give yourself an excuse for slipping from higher ideals into the dog-eat-dog mentality of the rat race. This is a good time to look in the mirror and ask that person what you are all about.

Lance expresses his vulnerability—his power—by being "honest, correct, and real" and by pursuing peak performance without fear. He avoids the empty rhetoric, phony intimidation, rationalizations, and finger pointing that are the calling cards of the weak and scared—those unwilling to be vulnerable. So the next time you are not at your best, instead of complaining or rationalizing about it, just accept it. Only then will you have a chance to do something positive about it. Life is not easy; bad things can happen when you least expect it. No matter how hard you try, you can't prepare or will your way to escape personal tragedy, depression, exhaustion, disease, plunging stock prices, and so on. Your only choice is to be vulnerable. Then, regardless of whether you win or lose or even get a fair chance to play the game, you preserve your character and your self-respect.

J.R. and the ER

We all have the opportunity to be champions even if our playing fields are more mundane and fewer than fifteen million people are watching us perform. You can be an anonymous champion by picking up trash or painting over graffiti in your neighborhood—yeah, even if you didn't make the mess! You can be a selfless champion in the workplace by pursuing the ideal of *doryoku* instead of putting self-glorification and advancement above all.

Linda Armstrong Kelly, she of many sharp tools in her shed and an extraordinary work ethic, nevertheless saw her career with big telecom firms unfairly sandbagged by official policies of not promoting people without a college degree and arcane antifemale (particularly single mom) politics. As she relates in *No Mountain High Enough*, on one occasion—circa mid-1980s in Dallas (think J. R. Ewing and his gang of darlin's or Dolly, Lily, and Jane in *9 to 5*)— she endured major grief for leaving the office during an intense deadline upon receiving word that Lance had gashed his toe and was woozy in the emergency room! Further stifling her climb up the corporate ladder, Linda purposely chose to minimize her responsibilities during Lance's formative years.

SO THE NEXT TIME YOU ARE NOT AT YOUR BEST, INSTEAD OF COMPLAINING OR RATIONALIZING ABOUT IT, JUST ACCEPT IT. ONLY THEN WILL YOU HAVE A CHANCE TO DO SOMETHING POSITIVE ABOUT IT.

Think that demonstration of priorities paid off? No, I'm not talking about the money Lance earned racing his bike. In fact, even when Lance hit the jackpot and Linda was busy managing things like construction of his new house, she maintained her career life in Dallas. "No, Lance has not supported me and I don't expect that at all from my son. That's just not fair to do," she told me.

Instead, she pursued a goal of "making my boss look like a million bucks." Sure, she eventually advanced and shined deservedly— after Lance left the nest and years of applied talent snuffed out the holes in her résumé. More important, she obtained fulfillment from expressing a passion and pure motivation for doing the best job she could, given the limitations of her circumstances and lifestyle choices. Particularly with the prevailing "me, me, me" attitude of today's rat race, this might be a hard lesson for many to grasp or implement.

"I was not one to compare," explains Linda. "Had I done that, I would have sunk a long, long time ago. Instead, I subscribe to the Golden Rule—'do unto others . . .' At the end of the day, I value and respect people and, of course, I want that back. That said, if I feel strongly about something, I will definitely express my opinion in a very diplomatic, professional way. If I felt I deserved something—a certain job or promotion—I always had the guts to stand up and ask for it. It didn't matter if I didn't have the education or hadn't been on the job long enough. I felt like I could contribute to the team, help my boss and others achieve goals, and create win-win situations. I loved the daily challenge of my career. It gave me a chance to wake up and make every day an opportunity."

Open House

Lance's Tour de France exploits are typically viewed as an end-all expression of his amazing talents. But in another dimension, the seven Mellow Johnnys are merely by-products of the application of tremendous character strength to a well-suited goal. Cycling enthusiasts realize the truth that Lance's victories were in very large part due to the command performances of his teammates, the magnificent mentoring and strategizing of Johan Bruyneel, and the helping hands of many others in Operation Lance Win Tour. But flipping that card over reveals that the strength of Lance's team was due in very large part to his outstanding leadership abilities. If Lance was an arrogant, selfish jerk, he would have won zero Tour de France titles (to those uninformed about Tour de France team dynamics and strategy—trust me, it's absolutely true), because he would not have had teammates who "would devote every ounce of energy in their bodies to work for Lance in his quest for the yellow jersey," as Mark Gorski observed.

Similarly, it's not good enough to succeed in the narrow dimensions set forth by today's rat race. If you are the number one agent at the brokerage for three years running but have left others in the office bitter over your devious tactics, or if you are disconnected emotionally from your family (open houses take precedence over having an "open house" of your own), you are spreading bad air in the world. Deep down, narrow performers—in sports, in business, or elsewhere—cannot escape the voids in their character. This leads to all kinds of amusing and destructive escapist behavior: the soulless obsession with wealth accumulation and consumption that many of those on the top of the food chain exhibit; the disregard for healthy diet, exercise, and lifestyle habits shared by those across all socioeconomic levels; and all the way down to the self-defeatist behavior and mind-sets of those who are struggling across the board—underperforming in career, in the family, and personally.

One More Chance

Bart Knaggs remarks, "We can always look at our shortcomings and retreat into our comfortable places. For example, I was the best basketball player at my elementary school, then one of the best in junior high, and then I started on the high school team for a couple years. However, I was not headed to the NBA. I retreated as the level of competition got higher. We can always make that choice to retreat. You and I can exchange e-mails where I lament that I'm out of shape, tired all the time, behind on all my work, not spending enough time at home, and all that kind of stuff. It's better to me to focus on the fact that I enjoy a very rich life. I require plenty of freshness and stimulation to keep me satisfied and at ease, so I continue to enjoy the pursuit of my goals."

What about you? Do you get off on freshness and stimulation, or do you prefer a level-two rut? If you've been fascinated and inspired to read and watch Lance extend the limits of human performance on a bicycle, that's great. Maybe you can leverage your inspiration to take action, discover your own fractal to break outside the box of conventional thought and behavior or your circle of comfort (or discomfort). Merely reading about and observing greatness, however, will bring you minimal satisfaction. Sure, you'll qualify for membership in your local dilettante club (meets at 11 P.M. every Thursday night at Starbucks), but you'll experience only 10 percent of the potential impact on your brain and body. You'll "retreat into your comfortable place," distinguishing yourself from peak performers in the manner captured by this classic quote from Theodore Roosevelt: "Far better it is to dare mighty things, to win glorious triumphs, even though checkered by failure, than to take rank with those poor spirits who neither enjoy much nor suffer much, because they live in the gray twilight that knows neither victory nor defeat."

As Lance says in *It's Not About the Bike*, "I realized that I only had one more chance [after recovering from cancer], and that this time around I had to do everything to the absolute maximum, to strive for perfection. This is my secret now. My competition cannot possibly have the eyes that I have." Each of us has only one more chance in life—today will come around just once in your lifetime. Make it the best day possible; do your absolute best today, tomorrow, and every day. When you adopt this powerful stance and act accordingly, you become a breath of fresh air to everyone you interact with in your life. Just like Lance.

INDEX

3 1143 00731 1203